FIELDWORK IN MEDIEVAL ARCHAEOLOGY

Fieldwork in Medieval Archaeology

Christopher Taylor

B. T. Batsford Ltd *London and Sydney*

ISBN 0 7134 2850 3 (hardcover)
ISBN 0 7134 2872 4 (limp)

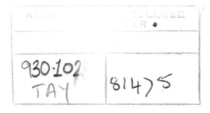

Filmset by Tradespools Ltd, Frome, Somerset
Printed by The Anchor Press Ltd, Tiptree, Essex
for the Publishers B. T. Batsford Ltd
4 Fitzhardinge Street, London W1H 0AH
B. T. Batsford (Australia) Pty Ltd
23 Cross Street, PO Box 586, Brookvale, NSW 2100 Australia

Preface

The methods outlined in this book are the ones which I have both used and taught over the past thirteen years with a fair degree of success. They are based on the thorough grounding in field archaeology that I was fortunate enough to be given by my friends and colleagues in the Salisbury office of the Royal Commission on Historical Monuments (England), and developed by work for the Commission in Wessex, East Anglia and the East Midlands.

In more practical terms the Commissioners, through their Secretary Mr R. W. McDowall, have allowed me to reproduce a number of drawings already in print, as well as to make use of material still unpublished. I am most grateful for this.

My colleague Hugh Richmond, has not only produced a number of valuable illustrations for this book, but has given much advice and helpful criticism which I believe has improved it considerably. Dr G. A. Webster has also helped in many respects and my thanks go to both of them. My greatest debt however is to my wife who has read and typed the manuscript numerous times, always improving it. Without her aid and active encouragement it would never have been completed.

C. C. Taylor

Contents

The illustrations

Acknowledgments

The author wishes to thank the following for permission to use photographs, maps and plans:

The Royal Commission on Historical Monuments (England) for figs 2, 5, 10, 11, 17, 18, 21, 23, 24, 25, 26, 30, 32, 34, 35, 36, 37, 39, 40, 43, 48, 49 and 57 (crown copyright reserved).

The Committee for Aerial Photography, Cambridge for figs 1, 6, 9, 22, 28, 29, 31, 38, 41, 50, 58 and 61 (photographs by J. K. St Joseph, Cambridge University Collection: copyright reserved

Cambridge Antiquarian Society for figs 23 and 27

Controller of H.M. Stationery Office for figs 20, 42, 44 and 45 (crown copyright reserved)

Council for British Archaeology for figs 46, 47 and 49

Wiltshire Archaeological Society for fig 59

1 Earthworks, Sywell, Northamptonshire
Now almost completely surrounded by modern arable is one small area of permanent grassland. It contains the earthworks of a former part of the village.

Introduction

Field archaeology is a term which has a number of different meanings. To judge from the contents of his well-known book,[1] Professor Atkinson would consider that it covered all types of outdoor archaeological work including excavation. Dr Coles, in a more recent work,[2] also sees field archaeology as including excavation.

Yet for an earlier generation of archaeologists the term meant purely the discovery, recording and interpretation of archaeological sites by visual examination alone, and without excavation. 'Field Archaeology' is said to have been coined by J. P. Williams Freeman in 1915, but this type of non-excavational archaeological work has a much longer tradition which goes back to Camden, Aubrey and Stukeley. In this century it has been refined by such workers as Williams Freeman, Hadrian Allcroft, Heywood Sumner, Leslie Grinsell and of course, the greatest of them all, O. G. S. Crawford.[3] Today it would seem that the age of giants has passed but field archaeology goes on, carried out by a host of people both amateur and professional. In this work we shall accept the traditional definition of field archaeology and not concern ourselves overmuch with excavation.

The limitations of simply writing about the techniques of field archaeology are self-evident. Field archaeology can only be taught and learnt *in the field*. To carry it out successfully needs considerable experience and a great deal of practice. It is not an easy option for archaeologists tired of digging, nor is it always a pleasant way of spending free weekends. Field archaeology is a specialised discipline in its own right which has a great and increasingly important part to play in the study of the past.

To write about Medieval Field Archaeology as if in some sense it is different from Prehistoric or Roman Field Archaeology is also fraught with dangers. There is no division, nor should there be in the mind of the archaeologist, between any period of history or prehistory. By the very nature of his work, whether he likes it or not, he has to deal with the remains of all periods from Palaeolithic hand axes to yesterday's ploughing. He cannot afford to specialise in any one particular period or one special type of site, for he is working to unravel from the landscape the sum total of man's activities over 10,000 years and more. He must be prepared to meet, record and interpret sites and finds of all possible periods and all possible purposes. He must also realise that, on any given site, human activity, whether constructive or destructive, can and often does continue long after its original purpose has been forgotten.

Thus the circular mound on a hilltop may be a Bronze Age barrow, or it may be the base of a medieval post-mill, or it may be both. Likewise the long low ridge, running for perhaps two kilometres across the countryside and passing under hedges, may be the agger of a Roman road. It is far more likely though to be a headland belonging to the medieval fields of the area, and it could be a combination of the two. There is not therefore, or rather there should not be, such a person as a medieval field archaeologist. There should only be field archaeologists who ought to be concerned with the totality of the past as it is revealed in the landscape in all its varied forms.

Nevertheless medieval field archaeology is worth examining by itself, assuming that the conditions noted above are always borne in mind, for it has its own special problems and techniques and in the last quarter of the twentieth century its own very special importance. While the general techniques of the discipline *in the field* are in many respects similar to those of field archaeology of other periods there is the additional factor of written records which can help in the discovery and the interpretation of archaeological remains of medieval and later times. While these records are of the utmost value, they require experience and care if they are not to muddle or positively mislead the unwary.

The importance of medieval field archaeology today is especially worth noting. We are now living during the period of greatest destruction of archaeological sites of all periods which has ever occurred, just when we are beginning to realise that there are more sites than we have hitherto imagined. The great majority of prehistoric and Roman sites have been ploughed over and damaged or destroyed in various ways. Many went centuries ago and we now only recognise them by scatters of pottery or soil and crop marks on air photographs. While the same destructive processes have also damaged or utterly removed many medieval sites too, these for various reasons have often lasted into this century reasonably intact and as upstanding earthworks. All over the country there are countless abandoned or shrunken villages, deserted hamlets, farms, moats, parks, gardens or agricultural remains as well as a host of other types of site.

The majority of upstanding earthworks now remaining are mainly of medieval and later date. Today these sites are being destroyed at an ever

2 The deserted medieval village of Kingsthorpe, Polebrooke,
Northamptonshire
*The remains of this village survived intact until the 1950s. Now only the hollowed
former main street survives. However field walking and survey have produced an
accurate plan of the site by plotting the areas of stone and pottery visible on the
ploughed land.*

increasing rate, and usually before their true nature has been recognised.
Already many sites are islands of earthworks in a sea of arable (1, 2). Much
has already gone, but much is left to be discovered. This should be recorded
and interpreted, either to be used as a guide for future excavation or simply
to make a note of its existence, form and probable purpose before it goes
forever. If this generation of archaeologists does not take this present
opportunity it will be lost for good. The remains will certainly not be there
for their children to see.

In this book we shall be examining the various ways in which medieval
field archaeology may be carried out and the steps by which it can be
achieved (3). These are not meant to constitute a handbook for the professional worker. They are to show the part-time archaeologist some aspects
of a side of his chosen field of study, which he can, and indeed must, take
up and so at very little cost and a great deal of pleasure record the vanishing
remains of a great part of our cultural heritage.

In the following chapters these various methods of work are illustrated
by many specific examples. The reader will soon realise that these are taken
from somewhat restricted areas of this country. This is largely because
I have relied to a great extent upon my own work which has, for professional reasons, been limited to certain parts of England. My motives for

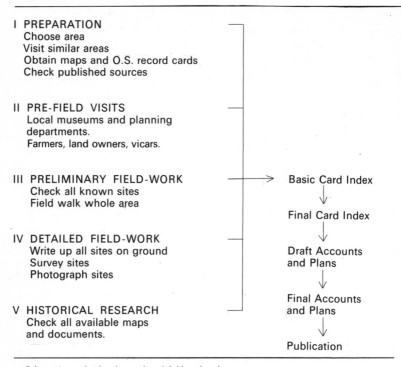

I PREPARATION
  Choose area
  Visit similar areas
  Obtain maps and O.S. record cards
  Check published sources

II PRE-FIELD VISITS
  Local museums and planning
  departments.
  Farmers, land owners, vicars.

III PRELIMINARY FIELD-WORK ——→ Basic Card Index
  Check all known sites
  Field walk whole area
                                    Final Card Index

IV DETAILED FIELD-WORK
  Write up all sites on ground   Draft Accounts
  Survey sites   and Plans
  Photograph sites

                                      Final Accounts
V HISTORICAL RESEARCH   and Plans
  Check all available maps
  and documents.
                                      Publication

3 *Schematic work plan for medieval field archaeology*

this are not that I doubt the value of accuracy of field archaeology carried out elsewhere, but merely that I am inevitably more familiar with these areas than others. In any case the geographical location of the examples is largely immaterial. They illustrate only the principles of field archaeology which are of universal application.

1 Preparations for fieldwork

Area

With any kind of fieldwork or excavation there is a temptation for the beginner to commence operations without sufficient preparation. But if really useful results are to be obtained, any serious work, either on a given area or on a specific type of site, must be preceded by a planned campaign indoors (3). This is necessary for a number of reasons. First one needs to think out very carefully what area of land is to be covered by the work, or what type of site is to be studied. Ideally intensive and detailed examination is needed and if too large an area is taken, or too many types of remains are included, there is a serious danger of effort being dissipated or only the most obvious discoveries made. For an individual worker one or two rural parishes, depending on their size, is probably quite a large enough area if he is to get to know in any detail every part of the land there. For a group of people, say ten or twelve, it is best to select five or six parishes as a start and as a base from which to expand.

To restrict one's work to a small area is dangerous as there is a very real chance of becoming too parochial. One may easily become so involved with local sites that they assume an exaggerated importance in the archaeologist's mind. The discovery of six new moated sites in a single parish may seem to be of vital importance. If the parish is one in central Hampshire, this hope may be justified. If it is in North Suffolk or Norfolk, the field worker will soon find that his discoveries are likely to be repeated in all the surrounding areas. The point is that the local enthusiast must plan his work to take account of the geographical and historical setting of a wider region than the one in which he is interested. He must allow time for work on this region by means of field visits to the sites there as well as studying the literature. Only in this way can he appreciate the significance of his work.

If it is desired to carry out field archaeology on specific types of site, he must include a much greater number of parishes. Here again he must try to decide what he wants and not be diverted from it. There will be temptations enough in the field, when he is studying deserted villages for example, to look at deer parks, castles etc. and this is not to be discouraged. The understanding of any one type of site can only be achieved by examining it in its total environment whether natural or man made. However if work is to proceed at a reasonable speed some concentration of effort on the chosen remains must be maintained. On the whole the study of a given area rather than a specific type of site is much to be preferred. Not only is it easier and cheaper for the field archaeologist, but the establishment of the relationships between the very varied sites likely to be found in the area and the rest of the environment, in geographical, social, economic and even political terms, is far more satisfying. Thus there is the need for a firm plan of campaign at the outset. As work advances and discoveries are made it can become more flexible, but the basic aims must be clear in the field archaeologist's mind from the beginning.

Maps

The next necessity in organising fieldwork is to obtain maps. These are absolutely vital to all stages of the work and without them little can be achieved. The purchase of a large number of Ordnance Survey maps may involve a considerable outlay, and this in itself is a good reason why a fairly restricted area should be chosen. The one-inch Ordnance Survey maps and their new replacement at 1 : 50,000 scale, while useful for many purposes, are totally inadequate for detailed fieldwork, but one covering the relevant area is necessary. Their most important value is that they usefully show public rights of way. The 2½-in. or 1 : 25,000-scale maps are by far the best. They not only show in detail accessible roads for cars, footpaths and all field boundaries but the 25-ft contour interval which they depict is normally sufficient to indicate the natural topography of the area. In addition the scale is large enough to allow generalised plotting of sites and even rough sketch plans of the earthwork remains.

These maps also show in various ways details of some sites that the archaeologist will be interested in, though the identification of these may not necessarily be correct. For specific areas and in order to show more detail, the 6-in. (1 : 10,000) or even 25-in. (1 : 2,500) scale plans are extremely useful. However it must always be remembered that enlargements of these plans to any convenient scale can readily be achieved by the simple method of dividing up the area of the site or field, on the map, into small squares. The detail of hedges and so on may then be transferred onto another sheet of paper already divided into larger squares. With care, the results are quite adequate for most purposes. Some field archaeologists have access to photographic equipment which can be used to enlarge Ordnance

Survey maps, though in this case, as the maps are Crown Copyright, permission to publish such copies must be obtained from the Copyright Department of the Ordnance Survey.

As well as the Ordnance Survey maps, the relevant one-inch-to-one-mile sheets of the Geological Survey ought to be obtained or at least consulted. In certain areas these are not published or are out of print but the necessary information can always be obtained by visiting the Geological Museum in London and copying the original survey information plotted on six-inch maps. The relevant geological sheet memoirs or Regional Geological pamphlets are also useful background reading. Though concerned with much that is irrelevant for archaeologists, they do help in explaining the content of complex geological deposits which are given rather general names on the maps. There are also, for a few areas, Soil Survey maps and Memoirs and it is always worth checking to see if they cover the region being studied. However, on the whole, the classification of soils on these maps is highly complex and based on chemical and physical differences which are not always understandable, nor relevant, to the field archaeologist.

Ordnance Survey records

Having obtained the necessary maps, the next stage is to start to collect information on what is already known about the area or the site. This again will save much extra effort and duplication when the actual fieldwork begins. There are innumerable sources which can be checked and as the work proceeds more will come to light. However the basic sources of information, which cannot be ignored, are the Record Cards of the Archaeological Division of the Ordnance Survey. These, together with the Index Cards, the bibliographical sources and annotated maps, are kept at the Ordnance Survey headquarters at Southampton. They can be consulted there if permission is obtained in writing beforehand. Another set of the Record Cards alone is also available at the National Monuments Record in London and these too can be consulted. The cards list sites and finds of all periods and include a bibliography, information from museum collections and individual local archaeologists, details of air photographs, as well as the results of field examination carried out by the Ordnance Survey's own field investigators. Thus it is an absolute necessity for medieval field archaeologists, and others, to have access to the information on these cards before starting work.

Even so, though these cards are a remarkable asset, they must not be regarded as either complete or infallible. They should rather be thought of as merely the starting point of future work. Other sources of information must be examined and checked. How detailed these checks need to be depends partly on what is on the Ordnance Survey Cards and partly on the accessibility of information locally. Ideally all the references on the cards ought to be examined, for there is no substitute for original accounts no matter how good the Ordnance Survey précis. However, the Ordnance Survey casts its net wide, and it is often difficult, if not impossible, to check every reference listed on the cards, which often come from relatively obscure national and local journals. On the other hand there is much information which the cards will not have and which can only be obtained by sifting through purely local and perhaps ephemeral sources. There is often a 'local history' written by a nineteenth-century vicar or schoolmaster, full of long manorial descents or detailed descriptions of church monuments. Most of this may be of little value or interest to anyone; but, on occasions, these older antiquarians note some discovery or give information of a kind which is worthwhile.

The information obtained from these sources, and others to be discussed in a later chapter, needs to be sorted and assembled in some form of retrievable system. Simply putting notes in files is not usually suitable, especially when as time goes on the amount of information grows. By far the best method is to build up a card index system similar to that of the Ordnance Survey Archaeological Division, as many other specialised archaeological groups have done. The Ordnance Survey Cards are based on the National Grid System and all sites and finds have a card which is identified by the relevant six-inch sheet reference followed by a number which is added consecutively to each new site or find as it is recorded. This works well when archaeological material of all periods is being assembled, though for a medieval field archaeologist it is perhaps more useful to arrange the cards by the parishes on which he is working. In rural areas at least these usually have a historical significance and are important when one comes to the interpretation of the material. However parish boundaries can and do change, and ultimately one must know the medieval boundaries in the area for the interpretation of the sites.

Aerial photographs

Aerial photographs provide another vital source of information which must be examined both before and during fieldwork. These can be divided into two kinds. There are those photographs taken for purely archaeological reasons and then the usually far larger number of photographs taken for very different purposes, but which are of great value. The latter are usually runs of vertical air photographs taken from a considerable height, each print overlapping the next by one third so that they can be viewed through a stereoscope. This produces a three-dimensional effect of considerable help to the archaeologist. These vertical air photographs include those taken by the Royal Air Force just after the Second World War. For many areas these are extremely important for they were taken before much of the modern destruction of archaeological remains by agricultural operations, urban expansion and road building of the last twenty-five years took place. They are thus already important historical documents in their own right. In more recent years various government departments, local authorities and other organisations have had similar vertical air photographs taken for specific purposes. Planning departments, river authorities, the Ordnance Survey and the Central Electricity Generating Board and many other bodies have had photographs taken of particular areas. The value of these for archaeological purposes varies considerably depending on the time of year they were taken and light, weather and crop conditions.

The air photographs taken for purely archaeological purposes are often oblique photographs. The best collection of these is, of course, that of the Committee for Aerial Photography at the University of Cambridge where amongst the tens of thousands of photographs taken by Dr J. K. St Joseph over many years are vast numbers of direct relevance to our study. As with the Royal Air Force vertical air photographs, the ones taken twenty or more years ago of sites, now destroyed by ploughing, are the only real evidence for the former appearance of many medieval sites.[1] In addition there are for certain parts of the country large and constantly growing collections of air photographs taken by amateur archaeologists and their friends.

The major difficulty with air photographs is gaining access to them, especially for the local worker. It is no longer possible easily to obtain copies of the Royal Air Force vertical photographs from the National Air Photograph Library, or indeed even to see them except through government departments. However many local authorities have sets of photographs of their areas and some, which have since obtained later air cover, have deposited the old ones in local record offices, museums or libraries. It is well worth the field archaeologist trying in all these places, and cultivating contacts in planning departments. In many cases it is usually possible to obtain permission to consult a collection.

Commercial air photographic companies too have large numbers of air photographs both vertical and oblique and these can sometimes be examined and purchased. Potentially the major source of air photographs will be that being built up by the National Monuments Record in London.

Already the material assembled there includes many Royal Air Force and commercial air photographs, prints of photographs taken by local archaeological air photographers and especially important pre-war photographs by O. G. S. Crawford and Major Allen. These again are now priceless as they record sites long since destroyed. As time goes on this National Monuments Record will become increasingly valuable and will be a major source of information for archaeologists of all periods. Once again, in most cases, permission in writing is needed before access to these collections will be allowed.

The occurrence of archaeological evidence on air photographs in terms of crop, soil, shadow and shine marks cannot be dealt with here. There are many useful books on the subject which ought to be consulted.[2] However, the interpretation of air photographs is not always easy and can only be successfully achieved with care and experience. Pipelines, wartime trenches, ploughing, cropping and tractor marks can often mislead the unwary.

Contacts with official bodies

In the preparation for fieldwork, a visit to the local museum is also to be recommended. Finds from the area being studied may be there, and in most, maps, card indexes, and correspondence concerning finds and sites are kept. In any case it is always useful to make and keep contact with the staff at local museums for they are usually some of the most devoted and helpful people in archaeology. Another useful contact which is too often ignored is with the local planning department. It is not always possible to build up the ideal relationship—it must be remembered that the planners are busy men concerned with many aspects of modern development. Nevertheless, because they are concerned with this development, they can often be of the utmost value to the field archaeologist. The overall plans for urban and rural expansion, and other changes as well as planning applications for specific sites can go a long way in helping the archaeologist to organise fieldwork and excavation. For example, in some counties, plans for all large-scale developments in rural areas are now passed to archaeologists by the planning authorities so that the site may be checked for potential archaeological material.

Local contacts

If the above method of work is being followed we ought now to have on our maps, cards or other form of filing a considerable amount of information on finds, sites, potential sites and proposed developments. All this will be useful when we come to make our own discoveries. However other contacts must be made before we begin work. The most important of these is to enable us to establish exactly who owns or leases the land over which the archaeologist must go. This is important for two reasons. First out of politeness and for the sake of both present and future workers in the area, the landowner's and tenant's permission must be obtained. It will help fieldwork a great deal if the areas of individual farms or properties can be fixed and perhaps put on maps so that the actual land ownership of all the region under examination can be ascertained.

Secondly farmers particularly often know their land better than archaeologists ever will and they can give details of earthworks, stone scatters and finds which might otherwise never be noted. This is especially true of land which has once been ploughed and then returned to pasture. The details of old ditches, now filled in, hedges removed and water and other pipelines laid, can often help the field archaeologist to pinpoint sites or reject likely crop or soil marks. Even details of cultivation techniques used on particular fields are useful, for deep ploughing with 'prairie-buster' ploughs can produce soil marks and even 'earthworks' which last for years.

Local farmers and other inhabitants can also provide a wealth of background information, and though much of it is likely to be garbled folklore about secret tunnels and the peculiar behaviour of monks and nuns, there is often a grain of useful information hidden somewhere. An investigation of the unlikely tradition in a remote Staffordshire village that a secret tunnel ran from an isolated copse to an abbey some 15 miles away led to the discovery of a small medieval homestead moat which was completely unsuspected. Even so traditional folklore and attributions must be treated with suspicion until proved correct. Many earthworks have acquired a doubtful respectability through their non-existent association with well-known historical figures.

A small bank, only 37 metres long and two metres high, which lies in the bottom of a valley in the parish of Broughton, Lancashire, is known as Cromwell's Mound, probably due to the embroidery of tales resulting from the Battle of Preston which was fought nearby in 1648. This has led to the identification of the bank as a seventeenth-century Civil War siegework. In fact it is only a dam, used to pond back a small lake. Its date is unknown, but the lake was probably a fishpond associated with a medieval moated site which lies not far away. Thus popular tradition and information must be discounted here.

On the other hand there are often local 'collections' of archaeological material in the hands of farmers and others which never pass to museums and which would otherwise go unrecorded unless the field archaeologist makes contact with local people. The great majority of farmers and land-owners are, if approached, willing to allow people to walk over their land provided they obey the normal rules of the countryside. It must be appreciated however that they are often suspicious of the strange breed of human beings known as archaeologists, sometimes with good reason. It is necessary to be as much a diplomat as an archaeologist if fieldwork is to be carried out successfully and one must be prepared to meet land-owners and farmers at their level of interests, not yours.

A very good means of acquiring useful knowledge, in order to smooth the path, is to listen to the B.B.C.'s farming programmes to keep up to date with agricultural views, techniques and problems. This always pays dividends. An hour spent leaning on a gate talking to a farmer about the prospects for this year's barley crop or the price of pigs in Shrewsbury market might be regarded as a considerable waste of time, but it usually helps in establishing good relationships for future work, quite apart from the broader educational value of the countryside, largely unknown to urban-bred archaeologists. The local pub too is an excellent place for making contacts and a source of information which should not be ignored, while vicars, postmen and roadmen also play an important archaeological role. So at last we should be ready to embark on the discovery of new sites by fieldwork.

2 Discovering sites in the field

If the careful planning advocated in the previous chapter has been carried out successfully there should now be a large amount of information on the whereabouts of actual or potential sites from air photographs, local knowledge, Ordnance Survey Record Cards and other sources. All these sites must be visited and checked on the ground. This will inevitably mean the rejection of some as well as the confirmation of others. Suspicious marks on air photographs may be where animals have been penned. Areas of stones may be where bags of seed potatoes from Scotland have been emptied and pieces of granite in them thrown out. The supposed 'ancient village' could prove to be a group of long-abandoned shallow gravel pits. On the other hand the local tradition of 'an old house in the wood' may be seen to be based on the existence of a medieval moat, while the record of sherds of medieval pottery on a museum map may lead to the discovery of building materials and other evidence of a deserted medieval farmstead. *

The checking of these actual and potential sites may take a great deal of time, but it has to be carried out. Unless the site is completely inaccessible or totally destroyed it must be visited at least once to confirm or reject the original source of information. No matter where this came from there can never be any substitute for eventual ground examination. The importance of walking over and around sites cannot be stressed too much as there is a temptation to neglect this in favour of the many aids to fieldwork. This is especially true of air photographs which often seem to show splendidly that which either still exists as upstanding earthworks, or which can be seen as crop marks. But even with these it is essential that the ground be walked in the end. If the ground examination reveals no additional archaeological information, which is unlikely, a field visit still gives an appreciation of the physical setting that no map or photograph can ever do. Slight undulations of the surface too low to show on a contour map, or even on a stereoscopically viewed air photograph, can often be of

* All these have happened to the writer during the course of fieldwork.

great significance. The apparently haphazard layout of a block of ridge and furrow seen on an air photograph is, when viewed from the ground, obviously the result of the acute perception by medieval farmers of the natural drainage.

A visit to a site gives a greater understanding of the soil conditions than can any geological or soil survey map, while the relationships of medieval fields to their villages, deer parks to the remaining woodland and moats to their water supply can all be better appreciated. Often an inspection can add greatly to the knowledge of a site already recorded. The scatter of sherds from a crop mark site, the establishment of a definite relationship between two earthworks or parts of an earthwork, only suggested by earlier workers or by air photographs, as well as much more can all come from ground examination.

Care must also be taken not to forget the most obvious places. Remains of medieval date, which are our concern here, will turn up in areas, or be connected with other features we are not directly involved with. The occurrence of earthworks within or attached to masonry castles, whose elucidation is mainly the sphere of the military historian, needs to be noted. The large earthen terraces inside the Outer Bailey at Corfe Castle, though still unexplained, have at least been recognised and recorded by field archaeologists, even though they form only a minor part of a huge and complex stone structure.[1]

From the known or suspected sites one must move on to the unknown. Ideally every part of a given area ought to be field-walked in detail, not just once, but a number of times over five or six years so that account can be taken of different crop rotations, agricultural practices and seasonal variations in the weather. This is unfortunately hardly ever achieved, but it should be the ideal at which to aim. This writer has achieved it once and then in only one parish over a period of five years, but the results were well worth the effort. The appreciation of the landscape in terms of man's adaptation to it over the last 1,500 years is a major achievement while the amount of purely archaeological material can be immense. Such work will of course not only produce valuable results for the medieval period but inevitably will produce sites of earlier and later times, all of which can be made use of by the good fieldworker.

A fine example of the kind of results that may be achieved by detailed field-walking in a potentially unrewarding area may be seen in the valley of the Lyveden Brook, west of Oundle in Northamptonshire. The area lies, not only within the great medieval Rockingham Forest on heavy Boulder Clay, but is also at the extremities of seven parishes. The existence of many medieval occupation sites in such an area would normally be regarded as unlikely, and Ordnance Survey maps show only two isolated moats there. However detailed field-walking by schoolboys from a local grammar school has produced a completely different picture. Over a period of some six years they have discovered two deserted medieval villages, one other large medieval settlement based on tile-making, two more moats, six medieval farmsteads and three post-medieval occupation sites. In addition eleven Romano-British settlements have come to light. Other workers have added one medieval deer park and an undated settlement which is probably prehistoric. This work has completely altered our ideas on the history of this valley and has made a very curious pattern on our distribution maps of medieval and earlier settlement of the region. Yet it is certain that there is nothing historically special about this one valley. It is special only because it has been examined in some detail by archaeologists. The same density of new sites is likely to be repeated all over the surrounding area.

In practical terms fieldwork is best carried out at certain specific times of the year. However attractive a long warm summer day in July may be for walking the countryside, it is not ideal for our purposes. Arable land should be visited when the ground is bare, or recently sown, and at this time the cooperation of farmers is more likely to be obtained as understandably they do not appreciate people wading through standing crops.

Work in mainly arable areas has to be fitted in with the particular cropping rotation. The best time is not directly after ploughing, but after harrowing, especially when rain has broken down the larger clods of earth and exposed and washed clean pottery and other debris. Walking can also be carried out after drilling or planting, in the few weeks before the crop starts to cover the ground completely. In areas where winter cereals are grown, investigation should be carried out in the late autumn, October to November. In fields where root crops such as sugar beet are being cultivated fieldwork may have to wait until December or January, while in areas where spring cereals or potatoes are grown it must usually be done in the first three months of the year. On permanent grassland, heath or moorland too, the winter or early spring are by far the best times, when the previous year's growth has died down and the new growth has not yet started. Winter too is always the most productive period for walking in woodland as it is the only time when one can move and see easily, especially in those old coppices which have been allowed to degenerate into near-jungle.

All this inevitably means that most work ought to be carried out in the colder and most uncomfortable time of the year when conditions, though ideal for field archaeology, are not particularly favourable for the field archaeologist. There are periods at other times of the year when work can be carried out in special circumstances. Though often a tragedy for the natural historian, summer fires on heath or moorland may present the fieldworker with a wealth of information, usually in the form of long-abandoned banks and cultivation remains or even occupation sites normally hidden by bracken or heather. When woodland is clear-felled, prior to replanting, and even after hay making, information can come to light. Winter weather, especially after a light snowfall, or when the snow cover has partially melted, produces ideal conditions for the recognition and identification of very slight earthworks as does low evening or morning light.

So, by following the countryside's routine and making use of the seasons, much material from new or old sites can be collected and assembled. Other activities too need to be noted and watched over. Any demolition or construction of buildings ought to be watched carefully if possible. This is particularly true in many villages. The gaps in between existing houses, where over the centuries buildings have decayed and been abandoned, are now being filled in with modern development. Observation of foundation trenches and other building activities can produce evidence of the older structures, their period of existence and perhaps date of abandonment. The demolition or restoration of older buildings can also reveal evidence of earlier occupation from under old floors and between wall footings. Pits dug for silage, electricity pylons, telephone poles, as well as the often more extensive road alignments and major road constructions, can all produce new archaeological material. In areas where large-scale extractive industries are located, such as gravel, sand, ironstone and stone quarries, long-term cooperation with the owners and staff of these works can be most productive.

One rapidly increasing activity of modern development which needs to be considered is the large-scale removal of top soil, excavated material and other rubbish and debris from one place to another. Over the last few years thousands of tons of material from urban development sites, motorways and smaller works have been sold and dumped all round the countryside to fill in old pits, make up new road verges and tracks and to improve poor land. Such material can and often does include occupation debris of all dates from the prehistoric to modern periods. Sometimes it can be readily recognised as removed material, but more often it can totally mislead the inexperienced. Great care must be exercised in this matter, and good relations with owners, farmers and farm workers can often help here in pinpointing and identifying such bogus sites.

All this work will eventually provide a mass of evidence for the medieval period, as well as for other ages. Much of it, especially in the early stages of the work, will be rejected. Subsequently it may turn out that the ancient looking bank around a small copse is a feature of nineteenth-century wood-land management, that the suspicious hole in the corner of a field is where a dead cow was buried, or that the mysterious platforms in a wood are the foundations of Second World War Nissen huts. But to note such features and to examine them is worthwhile as their ultimate recognition is neces-sary to distinguish them from other types of field monuments. In any case it is worth remembering that the human past which has left its mark on the landscape is not just of the period with which we are especially involved or interested, but everything that has happened from palaeolithic times up to this morning. It is worth repeating again that the good field archaeo-logist cannot afford to be a narrow specialist. He must be aware of the total history of the landscape, see everything, and if not understanding it at least appreciate its existence. Far too often there is a complete inability to see what exists and if the fieldworker does not use his eyes intelligently little will ever be achieved.

As this preliminary work develops the maps and index cards should gradually fill with information. At this stage much of it will probably be vague, such as notes of pottery scatters, low banks, water-filled ditches and possible old quarries. But all must be recorded, each feature with its exact National Grid Reference so that it can easily be relocated by others. At the same time pottery and other small finds will have been picked up from various sites. These must be treated exactly as an excavator deals with his finds. They should be washed, marked and stored in clearly labelled bags with a National Grid Reference to locate them. In this way, not only will there be detailed records for future workers to assess, but the investigator himself will be able to build up a useful working collection of pottery types and fabrics which may one day be of value in identifying local kilns and the distribution of their wares.

3 Recording in the field

Written descriptions

Having discovered actual or potential sites, the task is to record them, whatever they may be, in as much detail as possible. The need for detail is of paramount importance. It may well be that the investigator is the first person ever to see a particular site, and given the present rate of destruction, there is every chance that he will be the last. Therefore any record must be as full as possible for future reference.

A good example of the necessity for detailed recording is that of the common, though enigmatic, type of earthwork called the Pillow Mound. These were first noted and described by O. G. S. Crawford in Wessex[1] and subsequently they have been found all over the British Isles in every type of country and in every conceivable position. But even now, although we can be sure that they are of medieval date, we have no clear idea of their purpose, and neither excavation nor documentary research have enlightened us so far.

These mounds are characterised by being of rectangular shape, averaging 10–20 m. long and 5–10 m. wide, usually with a shallow surrounding ditch. They are always flat-topped and rarely more than 0·5 m. high. That is they are 'pillow' shaped (4). Though many have been recorded adequately, the literature is full of descriptions of long mounds giving height, width and length, but consistently giving no information as to whether the tops are flat or sharply ridged. Without this basic information, which is the most important diagnostic feature of Pillow Mounds, there is no way of telling whether most of these recorded sites are Pillow Mounds or not and all have to be rechecked on the ground, if they still exist. This may seem to be a minor point concerning an inconsequential type of archaeological site, but it does illustrate the need for the most detailed record of all medieval and indeed other remains.

Perhaps a more important illustration of this kind of detail may be seen in the recording of strip lynchets. These terrace-like features on hillsides are the remains of medieval strip cultivation. Normally the 'risers' or scarps bounding the strips were formed by plough action alone. But

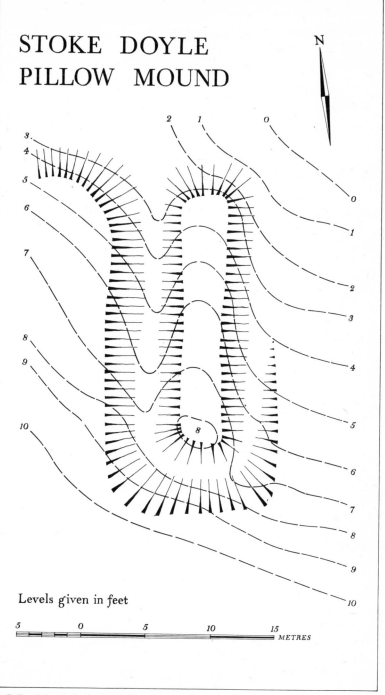

STOKE DOYLE
PILLOW MOUND

N

Levels given in feet

5 0 5 10 15 METRES

4 *Pillow Mound, Stoke Doyle, Northamptonshire.*

5 Strip lynchets, Bincombe, Dorset
The natural outcrop of limestone, projecting from the face of the riser, shows that these cultivation terraces were probably formed by hand digging before the strip ploughing commenced.

occasionally one finds natural outcrops of the underlying rocks projecting out of the riser face (5). The occurrence of such a feature is of considerable interest, for it indicates that the fields must have been partly constructed by hand before ploughing commenced. This then can give an insight into the kind of work that medieval farmers were forced to undertake when under pressure to bring more land into cultivation. Such evidence is not to be found in written records and only fieldwork can lead to its discovery.

The seemingly unimportant fishpond at Harrington, Northamptonshire, (6), also shows how much valuable information can be obtained if every detail of the site is examined and noted in full. Here, beyond the simple encircling embankment for the pond itself, there are inlet and outlet channels, overflow leats, earlier and later drains and other associated features. All need to be described as fully as possible.

By far the best way of recording sites is either to put the information on specially designed cards with suitable headings to remind the worker of all the details necessary, or to lay out the information in an established format. Amongst the former are the cards specially printed for the M5 Excavation Group (7) in order to enable a standard form of description to be attained along the whole motorway. These are an excellent way of recording such sites, though ideally the descriptions ought to be far fuller than the cards allow for. Longer descriptions of sites are best done using a set form of headings so that the same information is recorded on every site. A system devised by the Royal Commission on Historical Monuments (England) for its Investigators can be recommended here. This is the use of the so-called *tally cards* (*8*). Each archaeologist ought to carry one of these in the field, and note down all the relevant information under the headings laid out on the card. Ultimately it is possible to devise separate types of tally cards for specific types of site, e.g. one for deserted medieval villages, one for moated sites, one for mounds, one for cultivation remains and so on.[2]

As can be seen, the tally card has a number of headings, which may at first sight seem not to be directly related to the purely archaeological aspect of the site, yet all this information is relevant. Thus the simple bank, lying across a narrow valley at Silverstone, Northamptonshire, (*9*), and which is obviously a dam, needs not only a detailed description of its size and shape but of its overall setting as well. The shape of the valley in which it lies, the geology, probable area of the lake it once ponded back and much else, need to be recorded.

It may be argued that all this is not necessary, but it must be remembered that the newly discovered medieval moat which today lies totally isolated

6 Medieval fishponds, Harrington, Northamptonshire
The remarkable complexity of a relatively small area of land is well illustrated here.
The ponds themselves are only one part of a whole range of earthworks of many
periods.

in a remote corner of a parish may by next year have disappeared for ever under a vast new urban area, where all existing boundaries and other associated features have gone and even the original natural features such as valleys and knolls removed.

The actual details of a site, where it remains as upstanding earthworks, or even if it is merely a scatter of pottery and/or building material on ploughed land, must be as full as possible. Heights, widths, lengths of scarps, the exact area of pottery, and much else are all necessary. It is of little value to say that a bank is 'low' or that the pottery is scattered 'over a wide area'. The actual height of the bank to within at least 0·5 m. is needed as is the area of pottery to the nearest 0·25 of a hectare. It is not easy to estimate heights or areas. The former is particularly difficult and most fieldworkers consistently over-estimate the height of features but with practice these problems can be overcome.

It is also necessary to note exactly how many sherds of pottery have been found, for the interpretation of a site depends on this. Two or three sherds will mean very little. Almost every field in England will produce a handful of medieval pottery, probably carried out there in manure. Fifty to 100 sherds and other debris scattered over a few square metres probably indicates a habitation site. Too often fieldworkers merely note that 'some' or 'a quantity of' medieval pottery was found on a site. When questioned they say, if they can remember, that six or ten sherds were found. Such a number is unlikely to be of great importance.

7 *Standard record card used by M5 Excavation Group.*

Type of site	1	Period	2	County	3	Parish	4	5
Locality					6	National Grid Ref.		7
Description					8	Location of finds		9
						Visited by	10	Land usage	11
						Date		Date	
Bibliography, History File, Negatives etc.								12

270 CM/102 P&S

MEDIEVAL FIELDS

1 Classification: (strip lynchets, ridge and furrow etc.)

2 Location: (a) Maps O.S. 1 : 10000
(b) Boundary points with map references
(8 figures)

3 Situation: (a) Geology—from maps and as noted on ground
(b) Heights above O.D.
(c) Relief and drainage

4 Area: in hectares

5 Condition: present treatment of land

6 Features: (a) Whether arranged in 'furlongs' and how, details of occupation ways and other boundaries
(b) length (noting if full original extent or not), and shape in plan (noting if any reversed –S)
(c) height of lynchets or ridges, nature of divisions, baulks or banks?
(d) width, whether constant
(e) area of treads of strip lynchets
(f) slope of strips or ridges (if considerable) in degrees
(g) slope of treads of strip lynchets (if considerable), note if flat
(h) form of ends, 'cupped', run-out, headland, approach ramp, knuckled
(i) any structural features?
(j) any natural visible between risers on strip lynchets? any outcrops?
(k) relationships to other earthworks etc.
(l) any evidence of re-lay

7 Amplified description:

8 Initial documentation: (a) do the fields on modern maps preserve a recognisable strip pattern in the vicinity?
(b) do the remains fit into a strip pattern on Tithe, Enclosure or Estate Maps?

9 Nature of investigation: (a) detailed
(b) rapid

10 References: (a) plans made
(b) air photographs used
(c) ground photographs taken
(d) bibliography

11 Visited by: _____

12 Date: _____

8 *Check list or 'tally card' for medieval fields.*

The field archaeologist should walk carefully over every site with the record or tally card in his hand and whilst there note down all the relevant features and draw any vital sketch plans. The notes can be tidied up and rewritten if necessary at home, but if the details are not recorded as and when the fieldworker sees them, important information will be forgotten when he finally writes it all up, perhaps days or weeks after visiting the site.

Photography

As well as the written record, there should also be visual evidence. Every fieldworker must have a camera and photograph all he finds. Earthworks, especially very small ones, are notoriously difficult to photograph and scatters of pottery on a field almost impossible. The results are hardly likely to be aesthetically pleasing, and can rarely be reproduced in a learned article. Nevertheless they are valuable for giving a picture of the site which is impossible to achieve by the written record and often show the general siting and situation even if nothing upstanding remains. Once again they can help future workers to re-interpret a site after destruction. An example of this is the site at Upware in Cambridgeshire. It was destroyed in the Second World War, but it is still shown on modern Ordnance Survey

9 Dam, Silverstone, Northamptonshire
The great bank, spanning a small valley, is the retaining dam of a former lake. Its date is unknown.

10 Motte, Knapwell, Cambridgeshire
The lack of any scale in this photograph makes it extremely difficult to appreciate just how small is this twelfth-century castle mound. In fact it is only two metres high and 25 metres overall.

maps as a rectangular ditched feature and described as a 'Moat'. The fact that the original 25-in. O.S. map of 1886 shows it as a square mound and named it as such casts doubt on its identification as a moat, but it was not until an ancient photograph of a picnic party taking place on the site was found that its true origin became clear. The photograph showed that it was a mound, some 1·5 m. high with sharp angular bastions on the corners. It was a mid-seventeenth-century Civil War Gun Battery and not a medieval moat at all.

The technical details of photographing archaeological sites have been described elsewhere and the reader is referred to these.[3] Here it only needs to be stressed that, whatever is being photographed, some form of scale is needed. A human figure or a ranging rod, marked in metres, must be in the picture somewhere or when small objects such as building stones and other finds in situ are being taken, a small, clearly marked ruler calibrated in centimetres is necessary.[4]

A photograph without a scale can be positively misleading. The picture of a small eleventh-century motte or castle mound (*10*), already published in a state archaeological report with no scale whatsoever,[5] is an example of this. There is no obvious indication that the mound is only 26 m. overall, 2 m. high with a flat top 12 m. across. Yet this is important for some people would not recognise that such a small earthwork could be a castle mound. On the other hand the photograph of a simple moat ditch (*11*) with a human scale as well as ranging rods gives an immediate idea of the overall size and depth. Without these, particularly on a somewhat bare site, there would be no clear impression of exactly how big the feature was.

In addition photographs taken after a light snowfall, or when lying snow has partially melted, often show slight earthworks very clearly. This not only produces more valuable photographs but can be a great advantage in the actual identification of the earthworks themselves. Late evening or early morning low sunlight is also ideal for ground photography when even minute undulations in the ground can be thrown into shadow.

Sketching and surveying

Whatever a site may be, whether it is an upstanding earthwork or merely a scatter of pottery, it is essential that some form of plan, as accurate as possible, be made of the remains. This is to enable the later workers to perhaps interpret or reinterpret a site which the original fieldworker mis-understood. In this respect it has to be stressed that too often such a plan will be the only evidence for a site in the future. Whatever type of plan is made, it must be done *in the field* and not compiled later at home from a

11 Ditch, Caxton Moats, Cambridgeshire
The use of ranging rods and a human figure on this rather bare site give a good impression of the size of the castle ditch.

host of either rough, or accurate, measurements, jotted down on the back of an envelope. The finished plan must be checked on the ground when completed to make absolutely sure that it agrees with the actuality.

There are basically three ways of making a plan of an archaeological site in the field. At the lowest level, a simple sketch plan is better than nothing at all. This can take a very short time and even if wildly inaccurate at least shows the general layout and appearance of the site. As long as it is clearly labelled 'rough sketch plan, not to scale' it will add much to the available information.

An excellent illustration is that recently published from Sussex. By clearly drawn sketch plans a local archaeologist has recorded all the re-coverable details of two small deserted settlements, accompanied by a short text which describes and interprets both. The whole is a superb example of how to carry out this kind of work.[6]

Much better are properly surveyed plans, and these can be successfully made using the simplest of equipment, all of which is relatively cheap to buy and easy to use. The simplest plan can be made by compass and pacing. In this method a prismatic compass is used to obtain the bearings or angular measurements of each part of an earthwork and the linear distances are obtained by pacing (*12*). The average pace of any one person varies con-siderably and the field worker needs to check his pace beforehand by walk-ing along a measured distance. In addition one must also remember that when walking up a slope a pace is shorter than usual and longer when walking down a slope. However practice will soon establish what one's normal pace is.[7] With care, reasonably accurate plans of even complex sites can be made by this method. It is important to note on the plan the method used to enable other people to assess its accuracy and value.

By far the best method of making a plan is to carry out an instrument survey. The main difficulty here is not in the actual survey itself but in the mind of the potential surveyor. There is a basic and almost irremovable fear that archaeological field survey is complex, full of involved mathe-matics, and requires expensive equipment. This fear is not helped by the fact that the only books written on archaeological survey in general (including excavation sites) are full of complicated diagrams, mathematical formulae, cosines and tangents.[8] There is an urgent need for a short simple book on the elements of field survey finally to dispel this fear.

In this book there is no space to go into all the details of simple survey techniques, but perhaps a few words will help to guide the prospective surveyor. The average site that the medieval field archaeologist will need to survey is not large. Moats, windmill mounds, deserted farmsteads etc. are usually quite small and relatively simple. Even deserted villages or

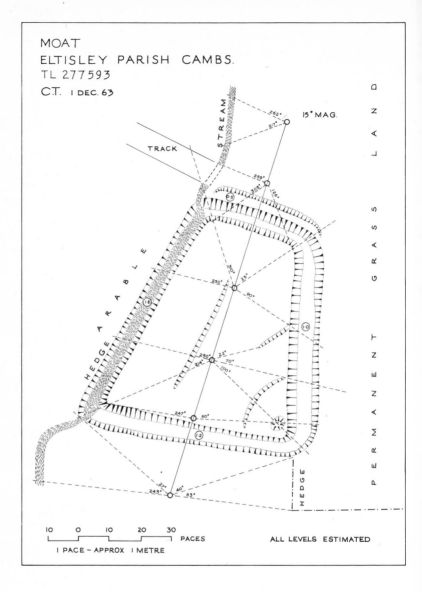

MOAT
ELTISLEY PARISH CAMBS.
TL 277593
C.T. 1 DEC. 63

15° MAG.

STREAM

TRACK

ARABLE

HEDGE

HEDGE

LAND

GRASS

PERMANENT

10   0   10   20   30
PACES

1 PACE – APPROX 1 METRE

ALL LEVELS ESTIMATED

——— BASE LINE
– – – OFFSET
–O– PEG POSITION

EQUIPMENT USED
   6 RANGING POLES
   12 MARKER ARROWS
   6 TIMBER PEGS
   2 30 METRE TAPES
   1 PRISMATIC COMPASS

0°–360°

12 *Field drawing of a survey, using a prismatic compass, of a medieval moat,*
Eltisley, Cambridgeshire.

shrunken or moved villages rarely cover more than, say, 4 hectares (about 10 acres), and are often considerably smaller. This is quite different from a 20-hectare hill fort, with all the problems of long distances and dead ground that such a site might involve. Occasionally one will come across large and complex areas of earthworks. Here, however, the site is almost always divided into separate areas by later hedges or walls and thus each part can be easily planned and later fitted together. Therefore in most medieval archaeological surveys we are likely to be involved in relatively small-scale work.

In all archaeological surveying one has to think clearly about the scale of the plan before starting and this involves deciding the actual purpose of the plan. On this decision depends the accuracy of the plan and the need for noting all kinds of details. The main object of a field plan is not to produce a large-scale drawing for future excavation on a small part of the site, though this may be required later, but a reasonably sized indication of the totality of the site. Therefore, however interesting it might be to do a large-scale survey of a deserted medieval village to, say, 1 m. to 50 m., and indeed however impressive the resulting plan might be when displayed, it is hardly in a form that can be distributed to other workers who might want to make use of it. The need for the work to be made available to other archaeologists is dealt with later on, but in the business of preparing for survey this need has to be taken into account at once.

All medieval sites ought to be surveyed with ultimate distribution in mind. In practice this means publication in one form or another. However one might wish to produce carefully surveyed plans in a pull-out folder in a national or local journal this is certainly not possible with present printing costs and usually is not worth it. Therefore one must make a plan that, *on reduction*, will take up no more than a whole page in a book or journal. Most journals for example have a page size, for print, of around 12–15 by 20–23 cm. If one aims for a reduction to about one third of the original drawing, the normal and best reduction, one must aim to get a plan at an unreduced size of about 60 by 30 cm. At this size a deserted village covering perhaps two hectares could not be surveyed at a scale larger than 1 : 1,000. On the other hand a small moat perhaps only 80 m. square, a windmill mound 30 m. in diameter or a single house site within a deserted medieval village could, if necessary, be drawn at 1 : 500 in the field. For most purposes, when anything except very detailed small sites are to be surveyed, it is rarely necessary to plan them at more than 1 : 500 scale. Most plans made by the Ordnance Survey or the Royal Commission on Historical Monuments of moats, deserted medieval villages, mottes and baileys are surveyed at 1 : 2,500, 1 : 1,250, or 1 : 500.

The choice of the scale for planning will immediately affect the amount of detail that can be plotted and, more important, the degree of accuracy. Thus even at 1 : 500 scale an average 2H pencil line will be nearly 0·25 m. wide and at 1 : 1,250 it will be 0·5 m. wide. There is thus no need to measure distances to the nearest centimetre or indeed to the nearest 15 cm. Added to this is the very imprecise nature of most sites. The edge of a scatter of pottery is a very subjective matter depending on how each surveyor defines what density of sherds makes up a scatter.

Even more difficult is where to fix the top or bottom of a bank or scarp. One can usually see the feature clearly enough but when one comes down to determining exactly where a low bank on a gentle natural slope ends it is possible to vary the point considerably. To prove this to a group of disbelieving students, the writer once made four separate groups plan a small and simple medieval sheep paddock. The results convinced them. Every plan showed the correct shape and layout of the site, with its entrance, bank and ditch and all the minor interior features correctly drawn. But they all varied up to a metre in places where the ditch and bank were not sharply defined. This inability in field survey to be absolutely accurate is the result of the nature of most sites. Combined with the limitations of scale noted above this not only lightens the work of the field surveyor but need not worry the beginner.

There are times when linear measurements must be accurately taken, but mistakes in plans usually occur not as a result of inaccurate measurements but as a result of errors in drawing. Having disposed of the necessity to be painstakingly accurate in measurement of distance let us now look at this problem of angles. When we are surveying a site we need to know the angular relationship of one feature to another as well as its linear distance. Except when carrying out a plane table survey, the only angles usually required are those at 90° (right angles) and 45°. Even then, these angles have no special significance beyond the fact that they can be easily established on the ground and just as easily drawn on the plan using a simple set-square.

On a small site, however intricate, no complex instrumentation or mathematics are needed. At the simplest all one wants is a method of laying out a line at right angles from a known fixed point on an existing line. This may be achieved in a number of ways. With a simple measuring tape one can construct on the ground a triangle whose sides are in the proportion of three, four, five units long. This, as those versed in simple geometry well know, makes one angle of the triangle a right angle. If this triangle is set on the existing line a right angle can easily be established. An easier method is to hold the measuring tape some distance from the existing line and swing the other end to and fro across the line. The point at which the distance along the tape is the shortest is a right angle.

Both these ways are good and accurate and may be used with effect in simple field survey. However if it is desirable to increase the speed of the survey another method using a simple and relatively cheap instrument can be undertaken. This is surveying with an *Optical Square* (*13*). This consists of a box, which can be held in the hand, or supported on a home-made rest. When the surveyor looks through an aperture in the side of it he not only sees the ground in front of him but, by means of a mirror set inside the box at 45 degrees, he also sees a view of the ground at one side. If he stands at a known point on a line and looks at a ranging pole fixed somewhere on that line the ranging pole is clearly visible through the aperture. If an assistant then takes another pole out to one side of the line and moves it about until one pole appears to be superimposed upon the other, the assistant's pole is then at right angles to the original line. Most small medieval sites can be accurately surveyed by this means, using no more than two measuring tapes, four ranging poles and the optical square.

In more detail the method is as follows. First of all a main 'baseline' must be established by means of the ranging poles. This line ought, if at all possible, to be laid across the centre or most complicated part of the site. This is achieved by setting three of the ranging poles in a straight line. If for example the site is a simple set of fishponds, unencumbered by trees, as in fig. *13*, the base line can be laid down the long axis of the site. At once, as this base line crosses a number of features the relative positions of these can be fixed by measuring their distances along the base line. Then by laying out a right angle from a measured fixed point on this base line, using the optical square or one of the other methods, and extending a tape along it, the archaeological and other detail which intersects this line can be measured. This line, known as an offset, can be repeated on either side of the base line as often as necessary to plot any other detail needed. Where there are either complex building platforms, curving banks and scarps or a number of irregularly shaped areas of stone or pottery, the interval between the offsets can be reduced.

This method is ideal on small sites and surveying can be quickly and accurately carried out, provided that the offsets are not too long. Thirty metres (or 100 feet) from the base line is usually the upper limit, for beyond this one cannot be sure that the right angle is exact, and a cumulative angular error will result in the misplacement of features.

The drawing of such a survey goes along as the actual measurements are taken of the site. Usually two people are all that are necessary to take these and a third can draw out the details. For those with finance or access

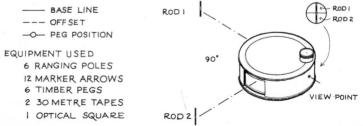

ABBEY FISHPONDS
SHAFTESBURY · DORSET
ST 864226
J.L.B 2/3/65

26° MAG.

HEDGE

ALL LEVELS ESTIMATED

10   0   10   20   30   40   50
METRES

——— BASE LINE
– – – OFFSET
–o– PEG POSITION

EQUIPMENT USED
   6 RANGING POLES
  12 MARKER ARROWS
   6 TIMBER PEGS
   2 30 METRE TAPES
   1 OPTICAL SQUARE

ROD 1

90°

ROD 2

ROD 1
ROD 2

VIEW·POINT

13 *Field drawing of a survey, using an optical square, of medieval fishponds, Shaftesbury, Dorset.*

to equipment, this can be done on an elaborate and expensive plane table fixed to a tripod. For most people a small drawing board or a piece of hardboard will do just as well. Cartridge paper, or better still, one of the modern types of plastic film, is taped, *not pinned*, to the board. Then the base line is drawn to scale on it. Using a set square the right angle offsets are drawn in from the base line and the positions of the details of the site are plotted on these lines and on the base line to scale.

The one disadvantage of the optical square or of tapes used in laying out right angles is that they permit *only* right angles to be laid out. In some cases it is helpful, more accurate and certainly faster to be able to lay out offsets which are not at right angles. This can be achieved by an even simpler instrument, *The Cross Head*. This instrument is not 'respectable' among professional surveyors, and is thus extremely difficult to obtain commercially. Nevertheless it is easily the best simple survey instrument to use on small complicated sites and various versions of it can be easily and cheaply made by the handyman once its principles are understood (*14*). It consists basically of a small round or octagonal cylinder which is mounted on top of a staff. The cylinder has a number of slits in it, each with a fine cross-wire for sighting purposes. These slits are carefully made so that each is 45 degrees from the other measured from the centre. So if the cross head is set at a known fixed point on a line, by looking through each slit, the surveyor can sight a line 45° and 90° in all directions. If the instrument is set up and sighted along the base line, six offsets, three on each side, two at 45° and one at 90°, can be laid out by putting ranging poles in their correct positions. Tapes can then be laid out along these lines.

This method, with its ability to fix 45° lines is very useful, as it means that much more archaeological detail can be plotted from each point and on a complex site it is considerably easier than the optical square. It also has the additional advantage for the field archaeologist who is a beginner in survey in that, used properly, it is self correcting and will even tell the surveyor when he has made a mistake in either measuring or in laying out his offsets.

This works in the following way. The surveyor sets up the cross head on the base line and plots all the features by means of offsets on both sides. He then moves the cross head along the base line, say 15 m. or 50 ft, and sets it up again. From this point, the two 45° offsets back along the base line will in fact intersect with the forward 45° offsets from the first point and also probably with the 90° offsets too. Therefore by measuring along these backward offsets the archaeological details already plotted can be remeasured and checked. If they do not agree, then the surveyor knows

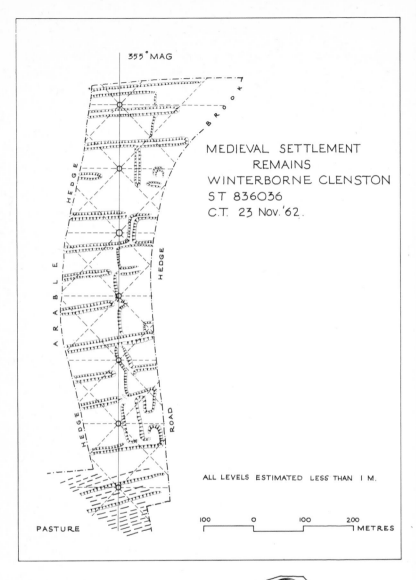

355° MAG

MEDIEVAL SETTLEMENT
REMAINS
WINTERBORNE CLENSTON
ST 836036
C.T. 23 Nov. '62.

BROOK

HEDGE

ARABLE

HEDGE

HEDGE

ROAD

PASTURE

ALL LEVELS ESTIMATED LESS THAN 1 M.

| 100 | 0 | 100 | 200 METRES |

——— BASE LINE
– – – OFFSET
–o– PEG POSITION

EQUIPMENT USED
   6 RANGING POLES
  12 MARKER ARROWS
   6 TIMBER PEGS
   2 30 METRE TAPES
   1 CROSS HEAD

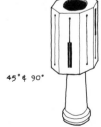

45° & 90°

14 *Field drawing of a survey, using a cross head, of the deserted medieval settlement of Philipston, Winterborne Clenston, Dorset.*

that a mistake has been made and he can find and rectify it before he has gone too far. By continuing the survey along the base line in this manner the whole site can be both plotted and checked. This saves the unfortunate situation developing whereby the mistake shows itself only at the end of the survey.

Though the cross head, as noted above, is now difficult to obtain, once the idea of having a simple method of taking angles from a fixed point is grasped, all kinds of similar home-made instruments can be devised, at a cost to suit every pocket. The Roman military engineer's *Groma*[9] may be resurrected and adapted for those with antiquarian interests. A real cross head can be turned on a lathe by a competent machinist, while for those with simpler tastes and abilities, a board nailed to a staff with sighting pins set at right angles and 45° will do admirably. This type of home-made instrument can be further refined so that intermediate sight lines and angles can be put in.

Another method of survey, preferred by some workers, is *Plane Tabling*. Unless the site is extremely simple, the normal method of intersection and resection plane tabling can be cumbersome, time-consuming and open to grave errors. The plane table is set up at one end of the measured base line which is then drawn to scale on the table. Having done this the table is then orientated so that the scale base line is sighted along that on the ground. The features to be plotted on the ground are marked by canes. Sight-lines to these are then drawn on the table using an alidade.* This completed, the table is removed to the other end of the base line and set up. The sight-lines to the same features on the ground are drawn in. The points at which these lines intersect mark the position of the features on the plan. However if the remains being surveyed are complex, perhaps a deserted medieval village with a large number of house sites and interlocking banks, the number of canes may be considerable and errors can easily occur. Moreover, unlike the previous methods where, at the end of the day the survey can be suspended leaving only a few pegs on the base line, when using a plane table the work has to be completed entirely or the veritable forest of canes left overnight. In an ideal world this may not matter, but in the practical world of field archaeology where cows and small boys take a particular delight in removing, pushing over or deliberately misplacing markers, it is much better to leave four small wooden pegs well driven into the ground and carefully covered over by grass, twigs or stones.

If the plane table is preferred—and there are advantages in it especially because it is more accurate over long distances—it is often better to use it

---

* An alidade is a simple device consisting of a wooden rule on which sight vanes are mounted at either end.

as a cross head. That is when a point is fixed on the ground and the table set up, as well as drawing the sight-lines in, a measuring tape is laid along the line and any detail that it intersects plotted. On complicated sites this reduces the number of points and sight-lines to be laid out, while at the same time establishing the details much more easily. By moving the plane table along the base line as with the cross head, other sight-lines can be used to check the accuracy of the earlier ones.

Up to now, in all the methods described it has been assumed that the whole of the site can be surveyed from a single base line, and indeed this is the case in the examples given (*12–14*). But many sites are of such a size or shape that it is impossible to reach their limits by measuring offsets from a single base line; secondary base lines must therefore be introduced. In order to position them correctly we use simple triangulation.

Once again, given the type and nature of the sites that are being surveyed and the relatively small areas involved, there is no need to lay out elaborate triangles using optical instruments. By far the best way is carefully to position a line at right angles to the base line and extend it into the part of the site that cannot be reached from the main base line. Then at a known point at the end of the new base line lay out a straight line of ranging poles sighted on a known point back on the main base line. The second base line and the third can then be measured and these lines drawn on the plan. It should then be obvious if a mistake in the measurements or in the original right angle has been made. When these lines are accurately plotted they can be used in the same way as the original base line, with the survey moving along them, taking offsets to various features. In this way the whole site may be covered (*15*).

These then are the simple and basic methods of field survey. By them all the necessary details of even complex small earthwork sites can be plotted in with considerable accuracy.

Let us now move on to the actual drawing of the details of a site in the field, for this usually causes considerable difficulties for the beginner. Assume that we have a simple bank and ditch to plan (*16*). From a point on our base line, by either optical square, cross head or alidade, we can sight across it and lay a measuring tape over it. All measurements have to be horizontal and therefore the tape must be pulled tight across the feature and not allowed to sag, otherwise a cumulative error in measurement will occur. With the tape correctly positioned, we have to note the point on it where changes of slope occur. That is we must measure the bottom of the bank, its outside top, inside top, the inside and outside bottoms of the ditch, and the top of the ditch. On our plan, we draw in the line of the tape and plot to scale the distances along it of the various changes

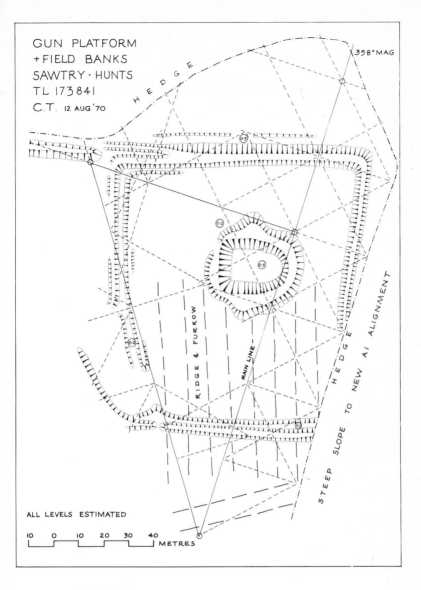

GUN PLATFORM
+ FIELD BANKS
SAWTRY · HUNTS
TL 173841
C.T. 12 AUG '70

358° MAG

HEDGE

RIDGE & FURROW

MAIN LINE

HEDGE

STEEP SLOPE TO NEW A1 ALIGNMENT

ALL LEVELS ESTIMATED

10   0   10   20   30   40   METRES

——— BASE LINE
– – – OFFSET
—o— PEG POSITION

EQUIPMENT USED
    6 RANGING POLES
    12 MARKER ARROWS
    6 TIMBER PEGS
    2 30 METRE TAPES

15 *Field drawing of a survey, using simple triangulation with a cross head, of a seventeenth-century gun platform, Sawtry, Huntingdonshire.*

of slope already noted. From the same point on the base line we may then lay out a new sight-line crossing the bank and ditch at another place, and repeat the process. Assuming that the bank and ditch are straight, we can then join up the bottoms of the bank, the two tops, bottoms of the ditch and so on. Thus we have established both the line of the bank and ditch, as well as the width of it at two points. The direction of slope can then be roughly marked in by small *hachures*, though their actual position and overall neat appearance do not matter at this stage. By repeating this method of marking in every break of slope on all the features of the site, the whole survey can be completed (*16*). Though not of direct concern here with the actual recording it is perhaps worth mentioning the subsequent stages in the drawing up of such a survey. The best method is to redraw the survey, leaving out the construction lines or offsets and sight lines, but copying exactly the lines joining up the measured points of changes of slope. This can then be redrawn by substituting neatly drawn hachures for these lines and for the crude hachures, and so produce the final plan (*14, 48; 15, 34*).

While in the field it is also necessary to do several other pieces of work. First, the plan should not be surveyed in isolation. Adjoining hedges, walls and existing buildings ought to be surveyed, so that the overall setting and relationships can be illustrated in the final plan. The plan should also be orientated correctly to north. This can be done by taking a compass bearing along the base line during the survey, noting it on the plan and later calculating and inserting true north. At the same time, the scale, national grid reference and name of the site should also be put on the plan.

One other point worth mentioning is that sometimes when making an accurate plan of existing earthworks it is advisable to omit features which might confuse the future reader or simply to plot them in a schematic way. This is provided that the extraneous detail has nothing whatever to do with the actual site being surveyed. Thus the neat plan, published by the Royal Commission, of the small medieval farmstead of Colber, near Sturminster Newton, Dorset, omits the fact that the entire field had been cut up by close set and deep nineteenth-century open drains which were in fact by far the most prominent feature of the site. If these had been planned, the overall picture of what the medieval farmstead looked like would have been completely lost (*17*).[10]

By the methods outlined so far it is possible to produce an accurate and detailed plan. But it is only a *plan*, nowhere have we made any note of the height of features. This often worries the new field archaeologist, who feels that the site should somehow be contoured. This is in a sense a justified worry, for, though the plan is of immense value, there must be some idea

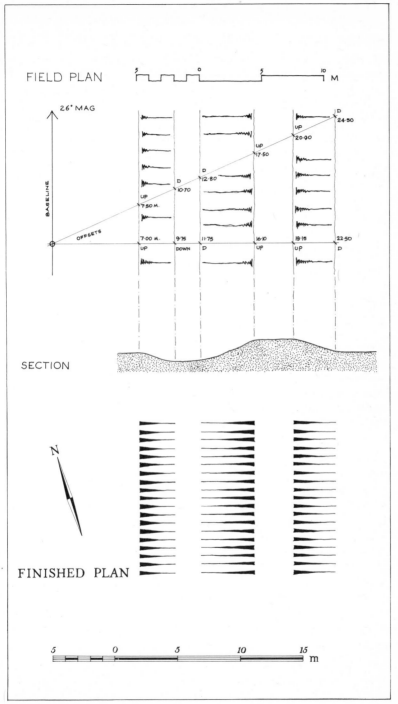

16 *Diagram to show the method of plotting and drawing breaks of slope using hachures.*

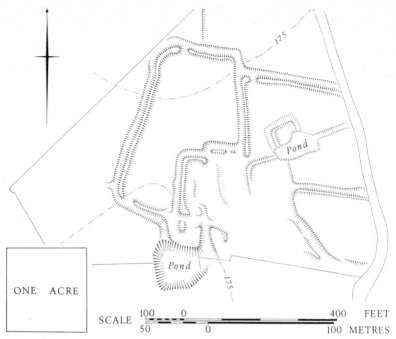

ONE ACRE

SCALE

| 100 | 0 | 400 | FEET |
| 50 | 0 | 100 | METRES |

17 *Deserted medieval farmstead of Colber, Sturminster Newton, Dorset.*

of the height of features as well as the overall natural topography. However in the majority of cases, detailed contouring of even a small site is not worth the time and effort spent on it. First of all such work involves a relatively expensive optical instrument which is not always easy for the beginner to use. Secondly, most medieval sites by their nature are usually extremely low, i.e. the average deserted medieval village rarely has banks or scarps more than one metre high. Therefore to make a contour plan, with the contour interval necessary to show any detail at all (i.e. a 10-cm. interval), would be immensely time-consuming. Even if this were done, the chances of it being meaningful are remote. Close contoured plans of low features, especially if on a considerable natural slope which will distort the feature, are virtually uninterpretable even by the experts. As an example of this, it is perhaps worth comparing the hachured plan of the seventeenth-century Sandhills Sconce at Newark, which took little more than an hour to make, with the 3-in. contour survey of the same site which took two days.[11]

There are occasions when it may be useful and instructive to contour a small mound of particular form, but even here it is best to combine it with hachures and both processes can be carried out together. Thus at a small Pillow Mound at Stoke Doyle in Northamptonshire (4) the hachures show its rectangular shape and flat top, while the contours indicate how it is skewed sideways across the natural ground surface, a typical feature in many such mounds. However it is usually much easier to record the height of archaeological features by other methods. The easiest is of course merely to describe in the accompanying report, that all plans must have, the height of each feature or of any particular part. For example one may say that the house platform 'a' on the plan is 0·5 m. high or that the bank 'b–c' on the plan is one metre high at 'b' and gradually slopes to 0·5 m. high at 'c'.

The other method is to survey profiles (i.e. the actual ground surface) of particularly important features, rather like an archaeological section without the below ground detail. There are two ways of doing this. The first is by using an optical level and a Sopwith staff. Most excavators are familiar with the use of this instrument and therefore it is not worth giving the details here.[12] The method can and does produce an accurate profile. However once again it is worth noting that the accuracy it gives is usually far more than is necessary when it comes to drawing out the profile. This must not have an exaggerated vertical scale and therefore even a bank 2 m. high and 5 m. wide will be less than 2 in. (5 cm.) high and about 4 in. (10 cm.) long when plotted to a ¼ scale, the largest usually necessary or possible. When this is reduced for publication to one third, it will be clear that the detailed measurements taken with a level and Sopwith staff are unnecessarily accurate.

Much quicker and easier, especially as it can be done single-handed, is to use a hand held level (an Abney Level or similar instrument). In this method the surveyor looks along a line of sight parallel to the ground surface and the angle of slope from the horizontal is shown on a calibrated scale. By measuring the distance along the ground a reasonably accurate profile can be made which is as reliable as that taken by the previous method when it is drawn out and reduced. The finished profiles ought to be added to the hachured plan, with their own scale clearly marked and their position on the plan itself labelled (*18*, *40*).

In addition to profiles and plan of a medieval archaeological site one needs a more generalised way of depicting the natural ground surface on which the site lies. It is important to show clearly whether it is in a valley or on a hill top. If it is desired, a rough contour survey of the area using a level and Sopwith staff can be carried out to show this. In this case with a contour interval of anything from 2 m. (5 ft) to 10 m. (25 ft), the task of contouring is not as difficult as with a very close contour interval. Even so it still represents a considerable amount of work and in most cases it is much better and certainly much easier to transfer the contours marked on

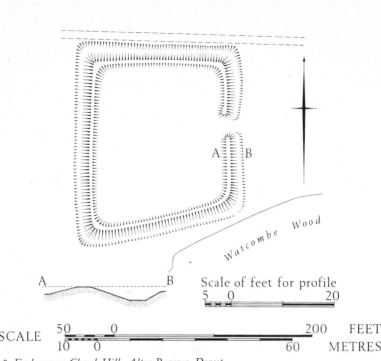

A B

Watcombe Wood

A .... B   Scale of feet for profile
                                                   5   0   20

SCALE   50   0   200   FEET
         10   0   60   METRES

18 *Enclosure on Church Hill, Alton Pancras, Dorset.*

the Ordnance Survey 6-in. maps onto the plan and, if necessary, interpolate intermediate ones by eye. This may be frowned upon by the purists and indeed it will certainly not be very accurate, but this is not important. At the present rate of destruction and the need for rapid survey we can hardly afford the time to contour precisely every site. Nor indeed is it necessary. The general contours on a field plan are meant not to reflect every minor natural feature, but to give an instant visual impression of the general position of the site.

Field walking

The methods of survey outlined above are mainly used for the recording of upstanding remains. Even when an occupation site is destroyed by ploughing it can still be surveyed, but the detailed methods already described are unnecessary. Such sites, which are usually marked by areas of pottery, building material and variations in the colour of the plough soil, can be quickly and easily plotted by field walking methods alone (2). Such remains may have been discovered during careful ground checking by the field-worker as outlined in the previous chapter. But a mere note that medieval pottery and building stone have been found at a certain national grid reference is by no means adequate. A more careful examination is necessary so that the actual area involved can be determined and any patterns which might indicate numbers of buildings or lines of streets can be established.

The first thing to determine is the overall area of the site. This involves no more than a fairly rapid walk around the area to discover its limits, though it is important to remember that a site may bear no relationship to existing fields and if one is found near the edge or in the corner of a field, the adjacent fields must also be checked to establish whether or not the site extends into them. Having found the general area involved it is then necessary to plot accurately the details discovered. This can be done by systematic field walking, an ideal task for a group of people. The first requirement is a plan of the area at a scale of at least 1 : 1,000 or even larger. This can easily be obtained by enlarging the Ordnance Survey 1 : 10,000 or 1 : 2,500 maps by the method of squares described on page 16.

Then a simple grid needs to be established over the area involved (*19*). This does not have to be accurately surveyed. A line of canes or sticks placed along the edge of the field 10 to 20 paces apart will do admirably as a base line and this is marked on the plan. Then the fieldworkers walk up and down the field at right angles to the base line, in line with the canes, plotting the density of pottery or stone and noting soil colour changes. The distances from the base line may be paced or measured with a tape depending on the size of the site and its complexity. If necessary the optical square and other canes can be used to establish the lines to be walked more accurately. In small fields, much detail can be plotted by eye using the positions and distances of corners, hedgerow trees or gates but in the increasingly large fields that modern agriculture demands this is not always possible. Often sites occur in the centre of huge prairie-like fields which have few or no reference points either on the map or on the ground. In these cases an arbitrary base line must be chosen and the work carried out from there. Later on it may be possible to fix the position of this base line by taking compass bearings to distant points.

The plans produced as a result of this kind of work can be of great value. Often much of the original layout of a deserted medieval village can be obtained from the density of pottery or stone rubble where no upstanding remains survive. The finds made during such field walking surveys are also of considerable importance. As noted earlier, all these finds must be washed, marked, labelled and bagged for they form a valuable part of the recoverable evidence.

All the foregoing descriptions of survey methods have been given to enable the beginner at medieval field archaeology rapidly and accurately to plan fairly small discrete archaeological sites. Deserted medieval villages,

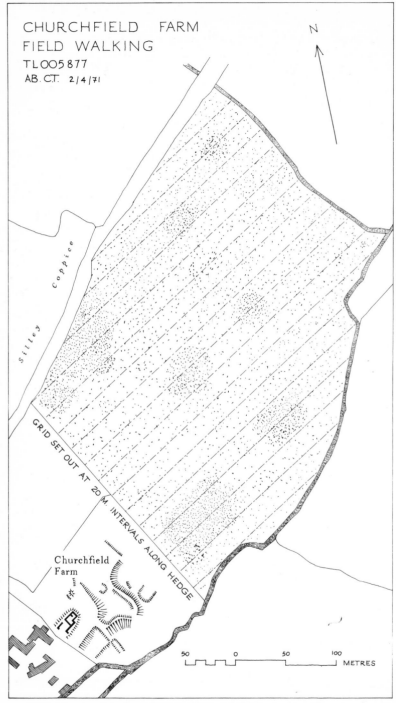

CHURCHFIELD FARM
FIELD WALKING
TL005877
AB.CT. 2/4/71

N

Silley Coppice

GRID SET OUT AT 20 M. INTERVALS ALONG HEDGE

Churchfield
Farm

50   0   50   100
METRES

19 *Gridded drawing of the deserted village of Churchfield, Northamptonshire,
showing the distribution of pottery plotted during field walking.*

shrunken or moved villages, small earthen castles and moats can all be planned by these means. Such work can also be used to show minor details within larger sites, such as individual house platforms in a deserted village, the entrance of a castle, a particularly interesting part of a set of strip lynchets or a block of ridge and furrow.

However there is also the problem of plotting rapidly other more extensive remains where only the general layout and shape are needed. In this category are ridge and furrow, deer park pales and linear boundary ditches. These features can usually be plotted by eye straight onto large-scale Ordnance Survey maps (*20*), though specific points of interest or important places of superimposition may require more detailed surveys. Many medieval deer park pales and other linear ditches tend to be followed by existing hedges. Where they are not measuring tapes may be laid out from known fixed points or even simple pacing employed. The same methods may be used when mapping blocks of ridge and furrow or strip lynchets. Large areas of ridge and furrow are more easily plotted directly onto 1 : 10,000 maps by using air photographs. At this scale individual ridges can be shown only as a single narrow line, but care must be taken to transfer accurately the detailed form of each ridge, so that the fact that it is straight, curved or reversed-S curved, or has marked kinks or bends in it is brought out. In addition the existence and width of headlands, division banks or ditches must be noted (*21*). All these have relevance when trying to understand the history of agricultural practices in the area being studied.

When this kind of rapid survey is being undertaken, there is always the chance of a more important earthwork being discovered. Thus in the middle of an area of ridge and furrow there might easily appear a low circular mound with a cross-shaped depression in its centre (*22*). This must not only be noted on the small-scale plan, but should be immediately surveyed at a scale large enough to indicate that it has the diagnostic features of a windmill mound, and that in this case the surrounding ridge and furrow is later than the mound itself.

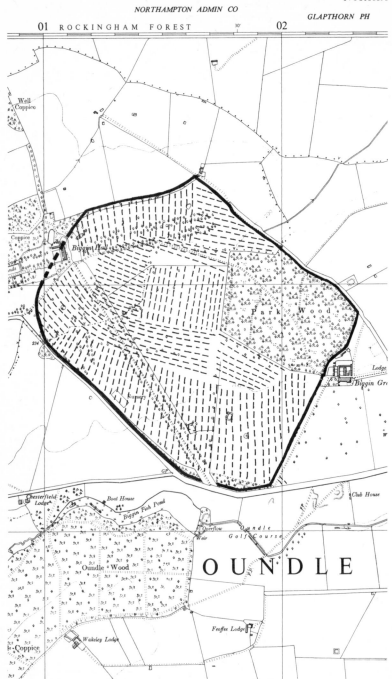

20 *Field drawing of medieval deer park and associated ridge and furrow, Oundle,*
Northamptonshire.

21 Ridge and furrow, Garton-on-the-Wolds, East Riding of Yorkshire
At the left hand side of the picture the ridge and furrow ends on a well-marked terrace which was both a trackway through the fields and a headland on which the plough was turned.

22 Ridge and furrow and windmill mound, Chipping Warden, Northamptonshire
The typical pattern of ridge and furrow, here partly ploughed away and underlying the modern hedges, can be clearly seen. The small windmill mound at the bottom right has a cross-shaped hole in its centre, indicating its original purpose.

4 Interpretation in the field

So far we have been concerned with the objective recording of medieval archaeological sites in the field. But the field archaeologist will have to make subjective judgements of interpretation all the time. Interpretation at this stage does not mean what a site is or what date it may be, but concerns only relationships of one archaeological feature to another or of archaeological features to natural and other man-made features. This is perhaps the most difficult side of field archaeology and certainly one which most beginners find the greatest problem. It must be said at once that there is no formula or easy way out of this difficulty. As with much else in field archaeology only experience and practice can ultimately produce the answers. Nevertheless there are certain guide lines to be followed and in this chapter we shall be examining these by looking at various examples.

Naturally most people new to this kind of archaeology will find the work of detailed interpretation somewhat frustrating, for at first they will not be able to see the often complex relationships that exist. But they must be recognised during the stage of actual recording or the written description or plan will lose most of its value. In addition the establishment of relationships is a vital part in the final elucidation of the site not only in terms of what it is or what it might be, but in the far more important aspect of how it originated and developed and what alterations have occurred. The main object of looking, particularly at upstanding earthwork sites, is to try to establish a relative chronology of the features that still exist.

At the most simple level, if when recording a block of ridge and furrow it is noticed that at one end the ridges are truncated or overlain by a railway cutting or embankment we have established a valid, if not very important, relationship. We can then be sure that the ridge and furrow is older than the railway and had either already gone out of use when the railway was built, or was put out of use by the construction work. Therefore a relative chronology has been established and in this case even an absolute chronology too if we know when the railway was built. The same applies to ridge and furrow which is cut by a road, or overlain by an existing field hedge. In this case the relationship is more useful, for the road or hedge may be of considerable antiquity. The precise date of the road or hedge is immaterial at this stage. This can be found out later on by other methods. Here, in the field, we can definitely say that our particular ridge and furrow was last ploughed at some time before the making of the hedge or road.

To take this simple relationship back further into the medieval period, two specific examples may be given. At Bentley Grange in the North Riding of Yorkshire there is a block of ridge and furrow overlain by a series of circular mounds, with deep central pits. At this stage of the simple field investigation it can only be said that the ridge and furrow is older than the pits. However, when later on these pits are identified as early medieval bell pits resulting from monastically controlled iron mining, we immediately have evidence of ploughing techniques in the area before the twelfth century and therefore a further examination of the ridge and furrow becomes important.[1] The field experience needed to identify the pits as bell pits, and the documentary expertise necessary to date them will come later, but if the relationship of the pits to the ridge and furrow is not recognised the value of the site in archaeological, agricultural and historical terms remains unnoticed and perhaps lost forever.

Likewise at Hen Domen in Montgomeryshire, the recognition that ridge and furrow ran up to and was cut by the outer bank of the motte-and-bailey castle, suggested that the ridge and furrow was earlier than the castle. This was subsequently proved by excavation. As yet the exact date of the castle is not known, though it must have been erected a little before 1100. Thus here we have ridge and furrow of the Pre-Norman Conquest period.[2]

The principle of simple relationship of ridge and furrow with later features can be used in other ways. In Cambridgeshire, south of Ely near Braham Farm, all Ordnance Survey maps show a rectangular enclosure 100 by 115 m., bounded by triple banks which are all under 0·5 m. high, with a simple entrance on one side (*23*). The site has interested local archaeologists for several years and many explanations for its possible use have been put forward, including a Roman camp and a medieval farmstead. The fact, actually of no importance whatsoever, that the adjacent farm is mentioned in Domesday Book in 1086 has also been used to draw attention to the 'obvious' antiquity of the enclosure. It has even been twice excavated with no finds or results. And yet until 1969 no-one had ever looked at the site carefully or made an accurate plan. Once this was done it was obvious that the whole enclosure lay on top of ridge and furrow which was still traceable within the interior and even between the

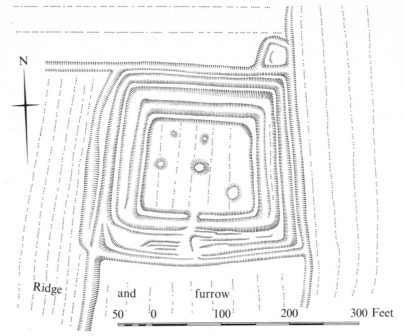

N

Ridge   and   furrow

50   0   100   200   300 Feet

23 *Medieval or later enclosure overlying medieval ridge and furrow, Braham Farm,*
Ely, Cambridgeshire.

enclosing banks. Thus whatever date it is, and this is still not known,
the site is clearly medieval or post-medieval, and whatever it was for,
equally unknown, it was certainly never occupied by buildings. The best
explanation is that it is a cattle or sheep pen of no great antiquity. The work
involved in establishing the relationships here took about five minutes
of careful observation and two hours of detailed planning; a great improve-
ment on the weeks or months spent before on excavation and the postula-
tion of unlikely theories.[3]

A rather different example of the relationship of ridge and furrow to
other features is to be seen near Yardley Hastings in Northamptonshire.
There a large bank, 150 m. long and up to 3 m. high, spans a narrow valley.
It is obviously a dam which once held the waters of a lake at least 10 hectares
in area. The date of the dam is unknown, and there is no direct relationship
between it and anything else. But on the valley sides above the dam is
ridge and furrow which ends just above the slight wave-cut platform
which still marks the former edge of the water in the lake. Therefore we
can be sure that the dam and lake existed when the ridge and furrow was
formed by ploughing. Once again the dating of the ploughing here is
difficult to ascertain, though it is probably medieval and certainly earlier
than the seventeenth century. But the recognition of its relationship to

the edge of the lake is a basic fact which can easily be obtained by careful observation.

The other form of medieval cultivation, strip lynchets, also provides many instances of identifiable relationships at quite a simple level. A particularly good example is the strip lynchets produced by medieval ploughing at Challacombe, Manaton, on Dartmoor.[4] There, later banks overlie and cross the treads of the strip lynchets at right angles and these are apparently associated with narrow rig plough remains usually said to be of eighteenth- or nineteenth-century date. Thus two separate stages or periods of agricultural activity can be identified. Elsewhere in the same area the strip lynchets are cut through by long running 'scars' or quarry pits, which are associated with nineteenth-century tin mining. Also at Challacombe are a set of embanked strips running down the hillside at right angles to the contours. These are fairly obvious but careful observation also reveals that there are faint traces of earlier strip lynchets running along the contours beneath them. Here is evidence, quite undated yet, of the massive alteration of a medieval field system which is rarely, if ever, recorded in documents. A similar example of alteration or relay is noted in Dorset.[5] There at Turnworth the lower ends of a set of narrow strip lynchets, running at right angles to the contours on a steep hillside, are cut off short by another block of strip lynchets running along the contours. Also in Dorset[6] at Ibberton, a group of strip-lynchets is crossed obliquely by existing hedges forming irregularly shaped fields. Within these fields it is still possible to see the ploughing marks which show that later cultivation was carried out across the existing strip lynchets at some time. None of these instances is an isolated case. They can be repeated all over the country and the careful deciphering of the pattern can tell us much about agricultural techniques for the last 1,500 years.

Moving on now to more complex examples and relationships we may take the deserted medieval village of Perio, near Oundle in Northamptonshire. Both the Deserted Medieval Village Research Group and the Ordnance Survey noted this site as unplannable earthworks only, when in fact a whole row of house platforms lining one side of the original main street exists. Apart from this, careful examination shows an important relationship of two features. The existing road past the site cuts across part of the original main street, now a holloway, and has destroyed all the house sites on one side of it. In view of the fact that no documents enabling us to date the desertion of the village accurately now survive, this relationship is valuable in giving us a *terminus post quem* for the abandonment of the village if we know the date of the existing road. This in fact is not known with certainty but it was already in being before 1600.

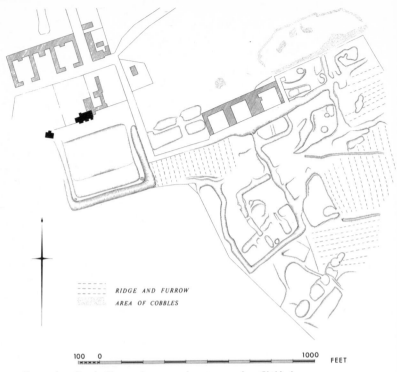

RIDGE AND FURROW
AREA OF COBBLES

100   0   1000   FEET

24 *Deserted medieval village and seventeenth-century garden, Childerley,
Cambridgeshire.*

Slightly more complex is the deserted medieval village of Childerley in
Cambridgeshire (*24*). Here detailed planning brings out the fact that the
main street of the former village, now a rutted holloway, is blocked at one
end by a rectangular feature bounded on three sides by a bank and ditch
and described as a 'moat' on Ordnance Survey maps.[7] It is inherently
unlikely that a normal medieval moat could have been constructed across
the main street of a contemporary village and therefore it is probable that
the 'moat' is not medieval at all but post-dates the abandonment of the
village. Once more, careful analysis of the moat reveals that it is in fact the
remains of a mid-sixteenth century formal garden, constructed at the same
time as the pretty Childerley Hall which fronts it.

A similar blocking of the main street of a deserted medieval village is
visible at Kirby, in Deene parish, Northamptonshire. Here a low bank,
only 0·25 m. high, with a shallow ditch cuts right across the existing
holloway. The bank can be traced for a short distance on either side, but
the rest has now been destroyed. Air photographs taken before modern
destruction show its continuation and indicate that it was the boundary of

a large paddock. But the photographs also show the bank cutting across the adjacent ridge and furrow. Therefore there can be no doubt that the paddock has nothing to do with the village and must belong to a period after its abandonment. In this case we know from a map that the paddock existed in 1584. But the map does not show the bank crossing the old main street and only field observation can accurately define its relationship. Also of course such observation, together with the map, gives us a clear indication of the period by which this part of the village had been abandoned.

Apart from these observable sequences of entirely different land use, fieldwork can also show the alteration and development within an occupied site. At the deserted medieval village of Bardolfeston, Puddletown, Dorset,[8] not only does an accurate survey show that the original main street is cut and blocked by mid-seventeenth-century water meadows, but more important it reveals two totally different layouts of the village, one superimposed on the other (25). The earliest layout as it is recoverable is a large L-shaped area of 6 hectares (15 acres) bounded by a low bank and subdivided into rectangular paddocks. The second stage is represented by a deep holloway cutting diagonally across the earlier remains, and bounded by some of the best preserved medieval house sites in southern England. Such a complete alteration is quite unrecorded in any document, and is not only of interest in itself, but adds considerably to similar evidence for alteration to deserted medieval village layouts discovered from excavations.[9]

25 *Deserted medieval village of Bardolfeston, Puddletown, Dorset.*

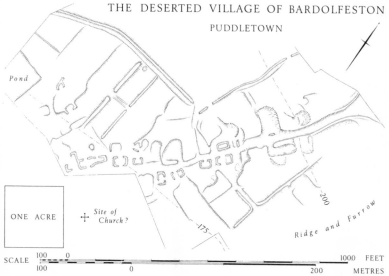

THE DESERTED VILLAGE OF BARDOLFESTON

PUDDLETOWN

Pond

ONE ACRE   + Site of Church?

Ridge and Furrow

SCALE 100   0 .... 1000 FEET
       100 ─── 0 ──────── 200 METRES

A different type of alteration is to be found at Huntingdon Castle. The castle, consisting of a motte and double bailey, has been planned and recorded in some detail. The published plan[10] shows incorrectly a wide approach ramp and causeway, carefully graded to a constant slope, which blocks the ditch of the motte and cuts through the top edge of the motte itself. But in fact the relationship of this ramp to the motte is very important (*26*). It cannot be contemporary with the early medieval use of the castle and therefore must belong to a later period. Likewise the rampart bounding the surviving bailey takes the form of a large bank 2–3 m. high and 12 m. wide except at one point. There it suddenly widens to 25 m. and is stepped up to a height of 4 m. This again is evidence of a deliberate heightening and widening of a short section of rampart, again at some time after the medieval rampart had been abandoned. Basic field observation tells us this and no more. However, long experience looking at earthworks of all periods suggests that the ramp across the motte is identical to ramps built in the mid-seventeenth century for dragging cannons onto a raised gun platform.[11] With this in mind, if we look carefully at the top of the motte we can see that it has a slight hollow with a low bank outside it. This same feature has been noted elsewhere on seventeenth-century gun batteries and explained as the result of digging in the trail to increase the range of the gun.[12] It thus appears that the medieval castle motte has been turned into a gun battery in the seventeenth century. The raised section of the rampart can then also be interpreted as a result of similar work to enable

26 *Detail of motte and part of bailey, Huntingdon Castle, Huntingdonshire, showing seventeenth-century alterations.*

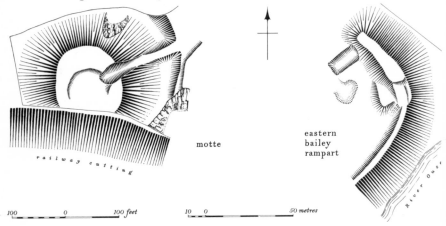

motte

eastern
bailey
rampart

railway cutting

River Ouse

100   0   100 feet   10 0   50 metres

cannons to be set on it and so cover the main river crossing of the River Ouse a short distance away. Further fieldwork around the town of Huntingdon has produced evidence of two other seventeenth-century siegeworks and with the documentary evidence of much military activity in the town, the initial field observation seems confirmed.

A similar picture of alteration and adaptation on another castle site is that at Castle Camps, in Cambridgeshire.[13] Here a low spur is crowned by a massive motte and bailey castle, built soon after 1066 by Aubrey de Vere, one of William the Conqueror's barons (27). As it remains today, it consists of a huge motte with a large trapezoidal bailey bounded by a high rampart and outer ditch lying below it on the slope of the spur. However inside the bailey are the much mutilated remains of another rampart and ditch, enclosing a very small area. This is all that survives of an earlier and probably original bailey, later abandoned and partly filled in when the castle was enlarged. Again no record of this enlargement and rebuilding survives and it can only be recognised on the ground. As a result, no date can be assigned to this enlargement but, though not very helpful, another observable feature at least gives us a *terminus post quem* for it. At one point on the line of the abandoned inner bailey ditch stands the parish church of the long deserted village of Castle Camps whose remains still ring the castle. This church cannot have been erected until after the castle was enlarged. Unfortunately the church today is the result of an almost total fifteenth-century rebuild, common in Cambridgeshire, which presumably took place long after the enlargement of the castle. A reset twelfth-century priest's door in the chancel may indicate that the first church was on the site by that time but this cannot be proved.

Nevertheless the existence of a standing building with a direct relationship to a medieval or later earthwork is not uncommon and the ability to date houses and churches is an often useful, if specialised, accomplishment for the medieval field archaeologist. Thus to note that a seventeenth-century farmhouse has been built over an area of ridge and furrow can help to establish the date by which the ridge and furrow was abandoned. This is important in areas where the enclosure of the medieval fields occurred at an early date and is not recorded in documents.[14] More specifically the ditch of a medieval moat at Malton, Orwell, in Cambridgeshire, is partly filled in and built over by a fine house of mid-fifteenth-century date, thus giving an indication of when the moat was finally abandoned.[15] Also in Cambridgeshire there is a seventeenth-century house on the edge of a former barge basin, used for medieval and later water-borne trade on the edge of the fens. The house is in such a position as to prevent the basin being used, and this direct relationship tells us something of the time of

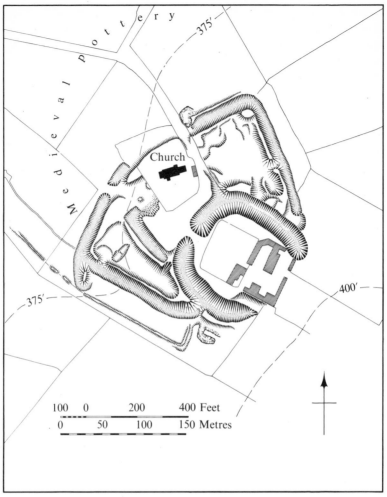

Church

Medieval pottery

375'

375'

400'

100	0	200	400 Feet
0	50	100	150 Metres

27 *Motte and bailey, Castle Camps, Cambridgeshire.*

abandonment of the basin.[16] In Dorset one of a series of massive artificial terraces at Milton Abbas, probably constructed for the cultivation of some special crop, has an eleventh-century chapel standing on it.[17]

Another important relationship is that between archaeological remains and vegetation. We have already noted the possibility of existing hedges overlying ridge and furrow and ultimately the date of that hedge may be obtained from documents. On the other hand the use of the new techniques of botanical hedgerow-dating and even bramble-dating may be useful here; a knowledge of simple botany is thus a most useful attribute for the medieval field archaeologist.[18] A small part of the history of the parish of Elmhurst, in Staffordshire, was revealed when it was noticed that an area of ridge and furrow was overlain by hedges which contained an average of five species of shrubs every 30 yards. This means that the hedges are approximately 500 years old and were probably laid out in the fourteenth or fifteenth centuries. The ridge and furrow therefore must represent arable cultivation before then. Though documentary evidence is not yet forthcoming, a working hypothesis is that this arable land was abandoned during the economic recession of the fourteenth century and that the new hedges followed as a result of sheep farming perhaps a century later.

A variation of this is the existence of old trees growing on top of earthworks. This can be a difficult problem for different species grow at different rates and size is not always an indicator of age. In addition soil and situation alter the growth rate of trees considerably. Dating of trees can be achieved by boring into the trunks and taking out a core as was done on the alleged remains of the abortive medieval town of Newton in Dorset. These were proved to be a group of post-medieval fishermen's cottages,[19] but this method is not to be recommended without specialised knowledge and supervision. Much easier and better is the counting of rings on tree stumps, whereby at least a rough estimate of the age of the former tree can be made and thus a terminal date for the abandonment of the site established.

The final problem in interpretating what we find and record in the field is the relationship between medieval and later earthworks and those belonging to earlier periods. This brings to the fore the question raised in the first chapter as to whether there can be such a person as a medieval field archaeologist. Of course there cannot be. The field archaeologist must be aware that all remains are part of the palimpsest of man's activities in the landscape. Very few prehistoric and Roman sites have remained untouched in later times and the recognition of these later activities and alterations needs to be appreciated by prehistoric and Roman field archaeologists. Thus many Iron Age hill forts have had their ditches ploughed at various times in the medieval period which has markedly altered their shape. One such is Bury Hill near Andover in Hampshire where the flat-bottomed ditches are the result of medieval strip ploughing within them. Likewise the cultivation terraces around the Roman fort at Housesteads, in Northumberland, which have often been described as Roman fields, can be seen actually to cut through the *vicus* and are therefore later than the Roman period. They are in fact quite normal medieval strip lynchets.[20]

In the same county the Roman fort at Chesters is overlain by medieval ridge and furrow, and indeed the survival of the rampart of the fort as an earthwork into the present century is partly due to the protection afforded it by the ridging technique of ploughing and the build-up of plough soil on the headlands which were laid out along the fort walls. In a different context, the low earthworks inside Yarnbury Hill Fort, Wiltshire, which have partly obliterated the rampart and ditch of the first stage of the fort are the remains of medieval sheep pens resulting from the great fair held there for centuries.[21]

Elsewhere the same alteration and mutilation of sites occurs and must be recognised. In Ashdown Woods, near Lambourn in Berkshire, a group of Iron Age 'Celtic' fields are overlain by a bank and ditch which is the boundary of a medieval deer park[22] while at the remarkable Romano-British native settlement at Meriden Down, Winterbourne Houghton in Dorset, another medieval deer park pale has been driven across the site, cutting 'Celtic' fields, roads and house platforms indiscriminately.[23]

A more unusual illustration of the medieval re-use of an older site is to be seen at Castle Bank, Cefnllys, near Llandrindod Wells, Radnorshire. There a small hill fort of just under two hectares has two medieval earthen motte and bailey castles within it, one at either end. By careful examination it has been possible to identify the features which are medieval from those which are of earlier periods. In addition, with a clear understanding of the military considerations of the site together with some fairly simple documentary work, it has been possible to establish a sequence for the erection of the castles.[24]

There is also the difficult but important recognition of medieval ridge and furrow overlying earlier 'Celtic' fields. The inability of an older generation of field archaeologists to see that the two types of cultivation were quite separate in time and relationship led to grave misconceptions as to prehistoric and Roman agricultural practices. It also led to the total ignorance of a whole piece of medieval economic and agricultural history (*28, 29*)[25]

The result of not recognising later occupation and alteration of a site is nowhere better illustrated than at Horningsea near Cambridge. Here in the late-nineteenth century, gravel diggers uncovered a group of important Roman kilns which produced the local Horningsea Ware. These were excavated and subsequent field walking resulted in the discovery of extensive Roman occupation of the surrounding area, including a probable villa. Later on, a large mound was excavated and though no structures were found, the vast quantities of Roman pottery discovered there led to the identification of the mound as a Roman building platform. Further fieldwork close by showed other earthworks, and more excavations there

28 Ridge and furrow overlying 'Celtic' fields, Compton Valence, Dorset

These two very different phases and types of ploughing need to be clearly distinguished if the agricultural practices and economy of the prehistoric and medieval farmers here is to be understood.

29 Earthworks, Ebsbury Hill, Wiltshire
In this photograph an Iron Age defensive work can be seen in the top left hand corner. In the centre is a Roman village, surrounded by its contemporary 'Celtic' fields. This village is partly overlain by a medieval farmstead and its fields have all been reploughed in medieval or later times. The large square depression is a nineteenth-century pond.

30 Moulton Hills, Bourn, Cambridgeshire
These mounds, though they contain Roman material, are of medieval date. Their purpose is unknown.

revealed an undated stone structure also claimed to be Roman. However the actual picture is that the undoubted Roman industrial site has a deserted medieval village on top of it, with holloways, house sites and paddocks, through which later gravel digging has taken place. The mound or 'Roman building platform' is in fact a spoil heap from the gravel digging while the stone structure is part of a medieval building on the edge of the original village street.[26]

The need for this kind of careful observation, related to older excavations, is a common occurrence. The three large circular mounds at Bourn, also in Cambridgeshire, which are up to 30 m. in diameter and 2·5 m. high have usually been described as Roman because of large quantities of Roman material found in them during excavation (*30*). But in fact the excavation, which took place in 1911, also revealed that there were medieval hearths on the old ground surface under the mounds, as well as medieval pottery and coins mixed up with the Roman material. While the actual purpose of the mounds is still unknown, there can be no doubt that they are medieval and are constructed from material which had been dug out of an earlier Roman settlement nearby.[27]

There is also the need to distinguish clearly the non-medieval parts of complex sites which may seem at first sight to be obviously medieval.

31 Earthworks, Denny Abbey, Waterbeach, Cambridgeshire
The abbey buildings occupied the farm in the centre. Around them lies a complex area of earthworks including fishponds, paddocks, drains and building platforms. The whole is partly surrounded by multiple linear ditches which are of Roman date.

Again in Cambridgeshire, the remarkable earthworks around Denney Abbey can be interpreted as the remains of fishponds, paddocks and building sites, all contained within a multivallate ditch system (*31*). This latter appears to be nothing more than the precinct boundary of the abbey grounds. However a detailed survey of the area, together with a knowledge of fenland Roman settlements, has led to the identification of the ditch system as of Roman date. This had been re-used, and thus preserved for posterity, by the medieval monks and nuns. The same feature occurs at the so-called 'castle' at Sturminster Newton, in Dorset (*32*). Here not only is there a respectable documentary history of a manor house, as well as a standing fourteenth-century structure, but there is also an impressive set of large earthworks including a bank and ditch cutting off a spur. However, once more, careful fieldwork has led to the interpretation of the site as a small prehistoric promontory fort, which was later used as a medieval manorial site.[28]

Occasionally there is a highly complex superimposition of many phases of activity. A fine example of this is at Ebsbury, near Wilton in Wiltshire. Here on a downland ridge are Bronze Age boundary ditches, 'Celtic' fields, an Iron Age defensive site, a Roman settlement, medieval ridge and furrow and strip lynchets, a medieval farmstead, nineteenth-century sheep ponds and trackways of every period, all intermingled and piled on top of one another. It takes the most detailed fieldwork, survey and long experience to separate all these features and put them into their correct chronological order (*29*).[29]

Modern alteration of medieval and later sites can also cause difficulties in interpretation if it is not recognised. The fact that two of the hut sites in a group on Tinkler Crags, on Askerton North Moor, Cumberland, are overlain by a large circular stone structure makes a considerable difference to the interpretation of these shielings. The circular structure is a nineteenth-century sheep-fold and therefore the huts must be older than the fold (*33*).[30]

So far we have concentrated on direct observable relationships of various parts of a site. But there is also the need to observe and to interpret non-relationships between earthworks. That is the recognition that adjacent sites need not be related to one another either in time or function. This may seem very obvious, but too often in the past and indeed still today this mistake is made. A nineteenth-century antiquarian identified as a Roman fort an apparent rectangular embanked enclosure, lying against the Roman Ermine Street at Stamford, Lincolnshire. In fact the 'banks' are a series of medieval ploughing headlands set at right angles to each other.[31] It is easy to scorn this identification but the same kind of misinter-

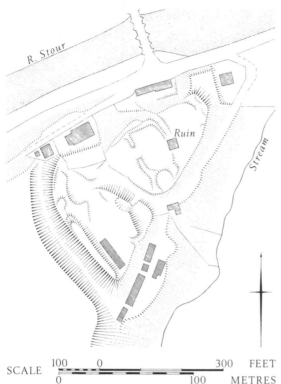

SCALE 100 ___ 0 _____ 300 FEET
0 _____ 100 METRES

32 *Iron Age promontory fort with medieval manorial earthworks within it,*
Sturminster Newton, Dorset.

33 Shielings and sheepfold, Kingswater, Cumberland
The well-marked circular stone structure in the centre is a nineteenth-century sheep
fold which overlies two earlier hut sites.

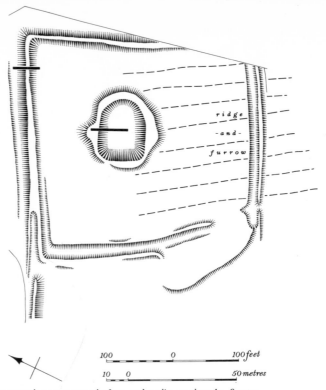

34 *Seventeenth-century gun platform and earlier earthworks, Sawtry, Huntingdonshire.*

pretation still goes on. The discovery of Iron Age and Roman sherds scattered on a spur above the River Nene near Irthlingborough, Northamptonshire, led to the identification of ramparts round this spur as part of a ploughed out 'hill fort'.[32] However these 'ramparts' are the remains of medieval plough headlands and can be recognised as such even on air photographs. Likewise the vast quantities of Roman pottery lying around some large earthen dams buried deep in a north Surrey wood led to the assumption that these dams were Roman. In fact they are most likely to be quite recent, perhaps seventeenth- or eighteenth-century in date and superimposed on the earlier site. This kind of mistake is only too easy to make when inexperience, keenness and an understandable desire to find important sites are fused in the mind of the archaeologist.

A more complex example of the care needed to notice non-relationships is to be seen at Tout Hill, Sawtry, Huntingdonshire (*34*). Here on a prominent rise, above the Great North Road and Roman Ermine Street, is a sunken embanked rectangular platform, surrounded by a large outer embanked and ditched enclosure. The discovery of immense quantities of Roman pottery nearby led to the suggestion that the site was a Roman camp or signal station. A trial excavation proved that both platform and enclosure were post-thirteenth century in date and further ideas as to their origin as a medieval farmstead were proposed. But when the site was surveyed carefully a number of features became immediately obvious. First, both platform and enclosure were seen to overlie medieval ridge and furrow. Secondly, the platform was not centrally placed in the outer enclosure and, thirdly, the platform itself was of unusual form, with one square end and one round, with the outer bank on only three sides. Finally the outer enclosure was not an enclosure at all, but part of a system of abandoned paddocks which stretch over a considerable area. Therefore the platform and 'enclosure' are not related. The platform, which can be identified as a mid-seventeenth-century gun battery, built to control traffic along the Great North Road, was quite fortuitously placed inside an old abandoned field for purely tactical reasons.

Likewise the long rectangular closes, which abut against the remarkable motte-and-double-bailey castle at Yelden, Bedfordshire, have no connection functionally with the castle at all but are part of the village of Yelden long since abandoned.[33] These examples are perhaps more difficult to recognise than the others since they involve a knowledge of types of earthwork in order to interpret the situation correctly.

Also associated with this general aspect of interpretation are the overall layout and shapes of earthworks. The importance of noting where ridge and furrow is C-curved or reversed S-curved has already been mentioned. But it is necessary to recognise such points as sharp bends or kinks in all the ridges of a block of ridge and furrow. These are often the result of reploughing as one adjacent and end-on blocks or furlongs, and are usually the only evidence for large-scale alteration of medieval agricultural systems.[34] A curious bend in a linear earthwork, say a deer park pale, may be the result of avoiding a now non-existent feature. Obviously field archaeology alone will not tell us what this particular feature was, but its possible existence needs to be observed.

The overall size, form, direction and geographical setting of linear earthworks of all kinds need to be considered. Though perhaps not of a scale that the average archaeologist will come across every day, the work of the late Sir Cyril Fox on Wansdyke and Offa's Dyke may be studied with value here.[35] The difference in size and appearance of the western end of Wansdyke from the main section is such that it is probable that the dyke here was built for a different purpose and possibly at a different date from the rest. Similarly the long gaps in Offa's Dyke are related to the original forest cover and thus occur where there was no need for a defensive work to be constructed. The same is true of the great Dark Age defensive

35 The Devil's Dyke, Cambridgeshire
This mighty Dark Age defensive rampart and ditch has been mutilated at this point by the removal of material for medieval road repairs.

work Devil's Dyke in Cambridgeshire which terminates abruptly on the fen edge to the north and on the margin of the former forest to the south (*35*). In these cases an appreciation of the present and former environment is involved.

The Devil's Dyke is also a useful example of how much close observation and interpretation can tell us about an apparently well-known site. The huge bank and ditch, facing south-west, runs for seven miles between forest and fen, and apart from two marked changes of alignment near its ends is always said to be exactly straight. But if it is carefully examined and exact compass bearings taken along it, a number of minor changes of alignment can be seen. These can be correlated with marked differences in the form of the bank and ditch and indicate how the bank was probably constructed by different gangs. In addition the marked bend in the dyke at its southern end, which was usually been said to be the result of the difficulty in obtaining a correct sight line over dead ground, can by examination of the natural setting be seen to be a clever and satisfactory way of improving an otherwise unsuitable tactical position caused by a deep dry valley.[36] Here there is the need to recognise the later alterations to the dyke, including quarrying for road metal (*35*).

The interpretation of earthworks also involves the analysis of minor details as well as broader aspects of relationships and non-relationships. Every site will throw up a host of problems of interpretation even after its general form, purpose and date are known. Thus when dealing with the earthwork remains of a medieval house site on a deserted medieval village, bounded by a bank obviously made of stone rubble, it is useful to make a judgement about the origin of the bank. Is it just the remains of a low wall footing or is it the spread tumble from a higher wall? A careful decision on this might tell us whether the house was originally built entirely of stone or of timber uprights set in a dwarf stone wall. Or when recording a block of ridge and furrow and noting that there are well-marked humps at the end of the ridges instead of the more usual run-out onto a headland, one must decide whether these humps could have been formed by the digging out by hand of the blocked adjacent furrows to assist drainage, or whether they are the result of generations of ploughmen cleaning their ploughshares at the end of each run. Both ideas have been put forward to explain these humps and only field observation can elucidate the matter.

A similar problem exists with strip lynchets. It is necessary not only to record the heights of the risers, widths of the treads and other obvious features, but to look carefully at the ends to see how the plough was turned when the terraces were being cultivated. Do they end in 'half round' curves, that is, is there a sharply defined curving angle at the back of the riser or negative lynchet where the plough has cut into it as it was being pulled round ready for the next run? Or do the treads become narrow and elongated to such an extent that some hand digging can be postulated on the site as well as normal ploughing? All these features can be seen on most blocks of strip lynchets and are well seen on those at Worth Matravers, Dorset (*36*). As with many points discussed in this chapter, detailed knowledge of all forms of man's activities both in the past and in the present is needed to make these decisions, and the aspiring field archaeologist will soon realise how much he needs to know of everyday life over and above his archaeological training.

So far in this chapter, although the function and date of the sites described have been given, no attempt has been made to explain how these facts

36 Strip lynchets, Worth Matravers, Dorset
This fine series of medieval cultivation terraces gives much information about ploughing techniques. The ploughing of the marginal land here indicates the shortage of more easily worked ground at some time in the past.

have been established. We have concentrated solely on the interpretation of minor details and relationships of sites rather than on the overall purpose or origin of them. This has been deliberate, for when we move onto this subject we approach the most complicated aspect of field archaeology. 'How do you know,' the beginner always asks, 'that this site is a deserted medieval village and that site is just recent quarrying?' or 'What tells you that this is a seventeenth-century gun battery and that is a medieval rabbit warren?'. The short answer to these questions is 'experience'. That is, years of practical fieldwork, a broad, open mind, capable of picking up all the aspects of rural life and retaining it, and a wide reading not only of archaeological literature, but that written by geologists, geomorphologists, botanists, farmers, art historians, architects, geographers, economic and social historians. This of course is no comfort to the keen beginner who wants to, and indeed must, get out into the field and start the urgent work of recording. Nevertheless the fact has to be faced that this kind of work is not easy and does require long practice to achieve total success. Even so the need for all these attributes must not be allowed to discourage the potential fieldworker. If he concentrates on the recording, surveying and simple interpretation of details and relationships he will be carrying out the most important part of the work. Ultimately by experience, or by documentary research to be discussed later, the answers will arrive, but the need to record comes first.

The understandable desire, having found a new site, is always to demand 'Well, what is it?'. If an obvious answer is not forthcoming, there is an unfortunate tendency to develop all kinds of fanciful ideas which usually have no relationship to the truth. Worse, but still common, is the usually quite unnecessary tendency to make a site more important than it really is. It is certainly disconcerting to find that the rectangular enclosure with curious gaps through its encircling bank, after being described, planned, photographed and even excavated with no result, should actually be a much mutilated fishpond, albeit medieval. It is much more satisfying to think that it is the site of a manor house, a civil war gun battery or Roman fort. Yet many sites have just this mundane kind of explanation which needs to be discovered and put on record. This is not only to distinguish them from the real manor houses, batteries or forts, but also in their own right as the remains of the activities and way of life of medieval people. Thus it is imperative for the archaeologist to temper his zeal with common sense when trying to decide what his newly discovered and highly prized site might be. Even then, particularly because of the additional advantage of documents that medieval archaeologists have over their companions who study earlier periods, any field interpretation needs to be left unproven until, if possible, there is confirmation or otherwise from documents or excavation.

Many small medieval earthworks can clearly be understood at a glance. Fishponds and dams come within this category (5, 6). But others of similar size do not. Apparently simple moats may be genuine medieval moated sites, but they may also be small castles (*10*), garden features of the sixteenth to nineteenth centuries (*61*),[37] or quite recent cattle drinking ponds. The two oval mounds respected by the adjacent ridge and furrow at Wold Newton in the East Riding of Yorkshire (*37*) would be quite impossible to interpret by either fieldwork or indeed excavation without knowing that they are called 'The Butts' and are recorded in 1299 as archery butts. And some sites remain completely unexplainable. The mysterious low earthworks just outside the castle of Caxton Moats in Cambridgeshire (*38*) are clearly connected with water. But their function and date are unknown though they do overlie ridge and furrow.[38]

For those readers who would still like to know exactly what their particular site might be, they are referred at this point to the bibliography where some of the sources for the basic diagnostic features of a few types of medieval remains are listed. However this is not the complete answer. To try to reduce the recognition of field monuments to a standard list of likely features can lead to endless difficulties. As Mr Fowler has already written on this problem, paraphrasing another worker in the field, ' "if you see" a rectangular earthwork enclosed by low banks "it could be" a medieval farm enclosure, just as well as a Bronze Age, Iron Age or Romano-British one. But then it could be several other things as well.'[39]

Even if a site has all the diagnostic features of a typical class of earthwork this does not necessarily mean that it belongs to it. On Chiselbury Warren, near Everleigh, Wiltshire, is a large group of earthworks which has all the features of a deserted medieval village. There is a deeply hollowed

37 Medieval archery butts, Wold Newton, East Riding of Yorkshire
These two mounds were first recorded in 1299 when they were being used for archery practice

38 Caxton Moats, Cambridgeshire

Though called moats these large and complex earthworks are the remains of a small castle of unusual form. The low earthworks in the bottom left, which have the unlikely name of 'The Asparagus Beds', are completely unexplained.

main street lined with the platforms of long rectangular houses, all set in embanked yards which also contain other building platforms. Surprisingly it is not a deserted medieval village at all, but an exceptionally well preserved Roman village.[40] Likewise in Cambridgeshire there are two almost identical low mounds, each some 30 m. in diameter and nearly 2 m. high, both with flat tops and surrounded by a ditch. One is a windmill mound, and the other a tiny mid-twelfth-century motte or fortlet (*10*).[41] The typology of earthworks, though having its uses, needs to be treated extremely carefully and certainly should never be used to prove the date or purpose of a site without additional evidence if possible. The blind use of form alone is nowhere better illustrated than in the identification of a host of similar earthwork enclosures in Wessex as being part of a supposed late-Roman pastoral farming organisation. When these were examined in detail the majority turned out to be medieval or later in date and included one fine enclosure for medieval rabbits![42]

Sometimes minor details of form and general geographical situation can be used to interpret quite simple sites. Thus many of the mounds marked as 'tumulus' on Ordnance Survey maps in Herefordshire can be considered as small medieval mottes, both from their steep-sided and flat-topped appearance as well as from their situation close to old farms or churches. Even an old excavation can help. The mound at St Weonards, Herefordshire, is listed as a barrow in the Royal Commission volume on Herefordshire. But its situation near the church, its form and even the evidence of an excavation section made in 1855 suggest that it is a small motte, not a barrow.[43]

If we then leave the final interpretation of the date and function of a site to the later stage there is still the problem of the actual identification of individual details. How do you tell the difference between a shallow hut depression and an equally shallow gravel pit? Once again this kind of problem can only be solved by practice and experience and even the experts can be sadly wrong at times. The earthworks in the centre of a Cambridgeshire deserted medieval village consisting of a large cruciform platform, orientated east–west, were confidently described as the site of a church. Yet subsequent excavation proved that it was the remains of a 'cobbled market place' and that the church lay just to the south.[44] Similarly recent excavations on deserted medieval villages have pointed to the possibility that the common shallow depressions found on such sites and usually interpreted as 'quarrying' are in fact stock yards.

Any interpretation of upstanding earthworks is fraught with such dangers and it is far better to say that one cannot interpret individual parts of it, rather than to try to explain everything in detail. Very often one cannot be

39 Village remains, Huggate, East Riding of Yorkshire
These well preserved and clear earthworks are the site of a single farm which consisted of a house and outbuildings arranged around a central courtyard.

certain whether the shallow depression is a house platform or a quarry. On the other hand if one looks *carefully* at a depression and it can be seen to have a rectangular form with marked right-angled corners, it is more likely to be a building site than indeterminate digging which is rarely rectangular (*39, 40*). If a raised level platform is also markedly rectangular it is more likely to be the remains of a structure than an 'island' left by shallow quarrying all around it. Similarly it should be possible to recognise with practice the difference between an original bank around the inside of a moated enclosure and the spread, somewhat uneven dumps of earth, formed by periodic cleaning out of the surrounding ditch, a process which may be quite modern.

When attempting to interpret earthworks, the fieldworker must also be careful not to confuse size of remains with importance or antiquity and thus see a site as older or historically more valuable because the earthworks are 5 m. high than another site whose remains are no more than 0·5 m. high. Most medieval settlement sites for example are usually very low and hardly visible, while those associated with medieval fields, in the form of strip lynchets, may, due to their position and length of cultivation, be anything up to 10 m. high (*36*). While features such as old trackways (*41*) may be, by their very size, obvious and impressive, they are only the results of traffic crossing open hill slopes over a long period of time, and as such are largely undatable and of considerably less value than say a deserted village or moated site.

The field archaeologist also needs to use all kinds of non-archaeological evidence in his work of interpretation. Vegetation can sometimes be a useful indicator of modern disturbance. The most characteristic is the occurrence of patches of nettles on a site. These often grow where ground has recently been disturbed by digging, and more especially if pigs or chickens have been penned there. The occurrence of common arable weeds is also an indicator of modern disturbance. It is important to notice the appearance of domesticated plants, whose seeds and roots have been thrown

40 *Deserted medieval settlement of Charlton, Charminster, Dorset; 'a' and 'b' are building platforms.*

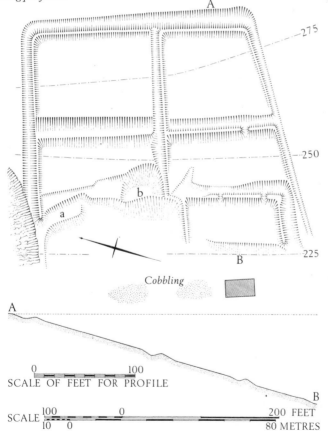

out with spoil to fill in holes. While the remains of modern bricks, mortar and concrete are easy to recognise as indicating modern disturbance, other refuse from the twentieth century is not so obvious at first. Such features as fragments of asbestos sheeting, widely used for roofing agricultural buildings and which look at first very much like pottery, or blast furnace slag, in some areas used for making up farm tracks, can deceive the unwary. Local knowledge from farmers and land owners may help here.

Often it is possible to establish by fieldwork that earthworks of apparently considerable antiquity are of no great age by noting the surrounding vegetation. This is especially useful when no early maps of the area under examination exist or when there is no other documentation. Thus the occurrence of very old and withered apple trees still standing within a well-marked earthwork enclosure on the edge of a Warwickshire village indicate that the remains there are probably the boundary of a garden still in use in the mid-nineteenth century.

The use of botany may be taken considerably further, though this involves perhaps a greater knowledge than the beginner might be expected to have. The occurrence of ridge and furrow in permanent grassland which has a rich ground flora is a reliable indication of a long period of pasture, thus providing evidence of considerable antiquity for the ridge and furrow. In a Huntingdonshire field, the existence of over 100 different species of plants, including large numbers of the relatively rare *Orchis morio* and sheets of *Ophioglossum vulgatum*, gives a clue to the great antiquity of the underlying ridge and furrow. *

A rather more complex example of the use of vegetation is on Lakenheath Warren in West Suffolk.[45] There is on the warren a series of rectangular enclosures, bounded by low earthen banks. Their date is quite unknown as is their original purpose, but they have apparently been ploughed at some time in the medieval or post-medieval period. The enclosing banks at opposite ends have been altered in shape by the turning of a plough over them. There are also traces of plough marks in the interior. This very slight evidence for ploughing is supported by a detailed examination of the vegetation in the area. For though there are no general differences between the vegetation within the enclosures and that outside them on the untouched heathland, there is a marked difference between the abundance of the various species in these two places. This indicates a recolonisation by the natural vegetation of the once bare interior in which some plants have been more successful than others.

Though we have already touched on the need for geological maps in

* This is a Site of Special Scientific Interest and therefore of considerable botanical importance, hence its anonymity.

41 Trackways, Postern Hill, Marlborough, Wiltshire
These impressive remains are the result of traffic climbing up the steep hillside, south of the town, over many centuries.

our work, it is also necessary to be aware of purely natural features in the landscape whose existence, though the preserve of the geomorphologist, needs to be remembered and taken into account. There are countless features which might seem at first sight to be man-made but which are actually the result of purely natural processes. Thus the form of some flat-bottomed valleys on the moors of the North Riding of Yorkshire is not produced by ploughing, even though it looks like it, but is caused by water overflowing from glacial lakes on the edge of an ice sheet. Likewise in all upland areas of the Highland Zone, well-marked benches or terraces on hillsides are as likely to be old river terraces or glacial lake shorelines as strip lynchets, while deep hollows on the faces of chalk scarps in Wessex are usually the result of periglacial action and solifluction rather than old tracks or holloways. The occurrence on heathland or moorland slopes of apparent ridge and furrow outlined by the vegetation must also be recognised for it is not the result of medieval farming on marginal land but the product of frost heaving in periglacial conditions causing stone stripes. Terracettes are another form of natural feature liable to be misinterpreted. These are tiny narrow terraces which often run parallel to or obliquely across the contours of steep slopes and sometimes cover entire hillsides. They are the result of downhill movement of surface soil under gravity often accentuated by animals walking along them. As such they have no relevance to our problems.

In the highland areas of Scotland, Wales and on Dartmoor as well as in some lowland areas there are flights of terraces on hillsides which may be mistaken for poorly developed strip lynchets. However these are altiplanation and solifluction terraces caused by frost heaving of the bedrock and down-slope movement. They can be distinguished from true strip lynchets for they do not have the sharp breaks of slope on the front and rear of the treads which ploughing produces and the risers, or scarps, are usually more uneven than is any strip lynchet.

Pingos or collapsed ice-mounds can also form circular depressions with an apparent 'rampart' around them which might cause confusion and there are a whole host of other periglacial phenomena which need to be recognised such as kettle holes and various pits, hollows, mounds and gullies, sometimes collectively called 'thermokarst'.[46]

Also open to misinterpretation are silted-up 'ox-bow lakes' or abandoned meanders of a river, which can look like battered defence works. Similarly the low, light-coloured ridges in the fenlands are not the result of either modern or ancient agriculture but are the former beds of streams now raised above the level of the shrunken peat as a result of drainage. Sometimes there is a combination of natural and man-made features. A volcanic intrusion or dyke, producing a hard rock band or ridge running across the countryside, after being quarried by man can look like a linear defensive work. The Cleveland Dyke in the North Riding of Yorkshire is an example of this. Even the apparently 'official' interpretation of sites can be shown as inaccurate by workers with a wider knowledge. Two mounds recorded in Herefordshire by the Royal Commission are almost certainly of glacial origin.[47]

At the other end of our time scale it is just as important to recognise the results of modern agricultural practices. Rolling grassland in spring produces a pattern very like ridge and furrow which can deceive the fieldworker on the ground as well as when using air photographs. Deep ploughing can actually produce shallow ditches and low banks while the pattern of soil and crop marks produced by the insertion of new land drains might also cause problems of interpretation.

All these examples are just an indication of the broad scope and interdisciplinary nature of our subject which ultimately the worker trying to interpret the evidence needs to be aware of. In addition to all this there is the other side of medieval field archaeology, that of documentary sources, which can ultimately provide many of the solutions.

5 Discovering sites by documents

The great advantage that the medieval field archaeologist has over his colleagues working on the remains of earlier times is that he is studying a period for which written records of various kinds have survived. This means that, by the careful use of these records, much more can be discovered and correctly interpreted about the medieval past than in the Roman or prehistoric periods. However the use and understanding of historical records is fraught with difficulty. Not only are they often technically hard to read, i.e. some at least demand a knowledge of medieval Latin or seventeenth-century Court Hand, but far more important they have to be understood in the historical context of when and for what purpose they were made, and whether we can take what they say at face value. There is an unfortunate tendency to accept the written word as the truth and to forget that written records, besides making statements of fact, also include the basic human aims of concealment, propaganda, prestige, greed and a host of other 'normal' aspirations. Therefore the use of documents has to be accompanied by careful analysis and a comprehensive experience of history in its widest sense.

In a book of this length it is impossible to list every kind of document which might be useful with all its accompanying problems of interpretation. We can only look at some of the principles involved. Most archaeologists may not want to delve deeply into the archivist's world, and at the best will only want an historian to provide them with information in order to find or interpret archaeological sites. In this and the next chapter we can offer only certain guidelines for both the archaeologist and his historian to deal with the material that exists.

First of all it is worth defining what we mean by documents. In the sense that is used here it covers all written records whether on parchment or paper, and includes maps, legal documents, newspapers, minute books, court rolls, photographic prints and engravings of any period. It also includes rather fewer mobile records such as gravestones and heraldic devices.

Modern maps

Large-scale modern Ordnance Survey maps and plans are documents just as much as the ancient manorial court roll written in indecipherable Latin and deposited far away in a record office. Indeed the modern map is likely to be of far more value than the court roll if it is used properly. This is especially true when we are concerned with the discovery of new sites. With experience the modern Ordnance Survey 6-in. and 25-in. plans are some of the most useful tools there are.

Basically modern maps, and indeed all maps, should be looked at for two separate things. Firstly specific features, which by their form are the results of hitherto unrecognised archaeological sites, or certain names which may also suggest the existence or former existence of sites. Secondly, patterns produced by fields, parish boundaries, woods, roads and footpaths which indicate an older land use of the area and therefore potential sites.

An example of a specific feature which may be of importance on maps is the occurrence in certain areas of L- or U-shaped ponds, often in small copses or in areas of woodland. These sometimes, though by no means always, can be unrecognised medieval moated sites whose other ditches are so damaged or silted up that they no longer hold water, or are too shallow to be marked by the Ordnance Survey. Thus it is only on recent Ordnance Survey maps that a U-shaped pond in a small copse at Whittlesford in Cambridgeshire, clearly marked on all earlier editions, has been described as a 'moat', which it certainly is. The fourth side still has its ditch, nearly 2 m. deep, but its recognition by the Ordnance Survey field surveyors was not made until a few years ago. Similarly on a remote hilltop, covered with heavy clay and almost impossible of access, in the Northamptonshire parish of Stoke Doyle, the Ordnance Survey 6-in. plan shows an irregular L-shaped pond (*42*). This was noted as a potential moat and careful scrutiny of the relevant air photographs revealed the other two parts of the ditch as a crop mark surrounding the original central island. A visit to the site confirmed this and led to the discovery of building material and medieval pottery there. As an additional bonus the ground examination also produced a small Roman site which, fortuitously or not, lay under the moat. Whenever such ponds are noticed on a map they should always be visited on the ground and checked on air photographs. Many will undoubtedly turn out to be cattle drinking ponds, old quarries or pits now flooded, or a number of other things, including perhaps medieval fishponds. In any case to see such things, even if they are not what one is looking for, is an invaluable experience in adding to the general understanding of the area being studied.

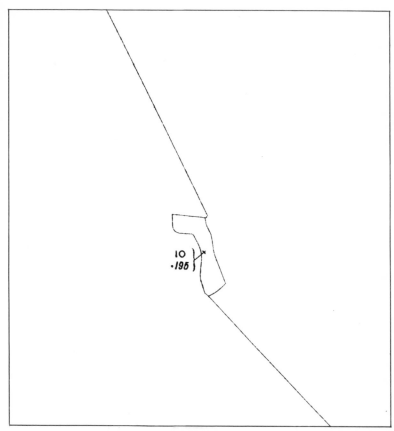

42 *Site of medieval moat, Stoke Doyle, Northamptonshire, as shown on Ordnance Survey 1 : 2500 plan.*

The value of just looking carefully at modern maps for the indications of such simple sites as medieval moats may be seen in the work of the Royal Commission on Historical Monuments in West Cambridgeshire.[1] The area was relatively rich in known moated sites, but nine out of the 63 moats finally recorded were discovered from checking unnamed pond-like features on Ordnance Survey 6-in. plans.

Other types of sites, both medieval and later, can also be discovered by looking at water courses and ponds shown on maps. Near King's Lynn in Norfolk a mid-seventeenth-century Civil War siege fort was found merely by noticing some angular bends in the open drains in an area of marshland. Ground examination proved that these were the result of the modern drains following the line of the angle bastions, characteristic of seventeenth-century fortification. Elsewhere in the fenlands of Eastern England the history of the drainage of these fens can be considerably aided by establishing the whereabouts of the old windpumps which until the nineteenth century were the basic way of lifting water out of the fens. None of these now survives as a standing structure, but the positions of literally hundreds of them can be identified on modern maps by the characteristic arrangement of their approach drains or reservoirs which usually still exist, though now used for other purposes (*43*).[2]

From an earlier period, abandoned medieval watermills often leave characteristic features which are marked on maps. At Dewlish, in Dorset, the Ordnance Survey 6-in. plan shows a curious sharp double bend in an otherwise gently meandering stream flowing down the narrow chalk-cut valley. A field visit to check this suspicious feature showed that it was caused by the stream being diverted into a later channel cut through a huge earthen dam, 60 m. long, 12 m. wide and 2 m. high, which no-one had recorded. Further examination produced the building platform of the mill which was worked by the water ponded behind the dam, and later documentary work pointed to the fact that the mill was in existence by the early fourteenth century.[3]

A very common feature on maps, well worth checking in certain areas, is the isolated church, or church set some distance away from an existing village. This feature needs to be used with some care, but over most of lowland Britain at least it often indicates deserted, shrunken or shifted villages, and evidence of former buildings and roads or at least scatters of pottery and building materials often survive. Thus at Caxton in Cambridgeshire even the 1-in. map shows that while the modern village now lies on either side of the Old North Road, once the Roman Ermine Street, the church stands a quarter of a mile away, virtually alone except for two farms. However, as ground checking shows, around the church are a number of disused holloways and areas of early medieval pottery, from which we may deduce that the original village lay here and subsequently moved away to the main road (*62*).[4] The classic case, well known to most people, is of course at Wharram Percy, in the East Riding of Yorkshire, where an isolated church has a remarkably fine deserted village around it.[5] Countless other examples exist.

However, an isolated church is not always proof of a moved or deserted settlement. In the highland zone of this country, especially in south west England, Wales and the north where isolated churches are relatively common, these churches result from an older probably Celtic pattern of

43 Site of Windpump, Horningsea, Cambridgeshire
*The shallow rectangular depression in the middle of the fens is the reservoir of a
former windpump. This was built in the early nineteenth century to lift water from
the surrounding land and throw it into the high level drain on the left of the picture.*

settlement, where they were not necessarily in or indeed near a village.
In some of these areas, villages as most people know them did not exist
at all until relatively recent times. The same is said to be true of parts of
East Anglia, especially Norfolk, though recent work has suggested that
there were indeed once villages around the many now isolated churches.
In other places too an isolated church may not necessarily indicate desertion or movement. A very good example is at Knowlton in Dorset where
the now ruined twelfth-century church stands in the centre of a Neolithic
henge monument. For generations local historians and archaeologists have
looked for the site of the village of Knowlton on the assumption that it
lay near its church. However the earthwork remains of the village were
actually discovered some distance away on the edge of the River Allen in
exactly the same situation as all the existing villages in the area. The church
stands on a site which had probably been continually used for ritual purposes from the Neolithic period onwards. The church at Maxey in South
Lincolnshire, which also stands on a large mound, quite isolated from the
existing village, has no trace of an earlier village near it. Again in an area
of intensive prehistoric and Roman occupation, it perhaps reflects the
continuing ritual significance of its site from pagan times into the Christian
era.[6]

Stow Church, in Cambridgeshire, lies apart from its village on a low
hill (*44*). Again many people have searched for the remains of the original
village of Stow around it, but have found nothing. Here the very name

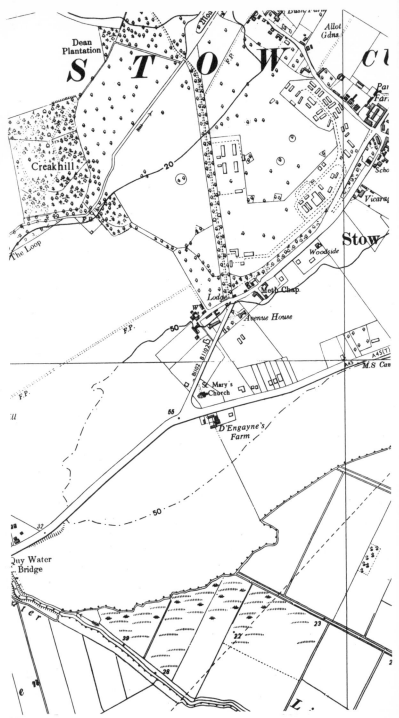

44 *Ordnance Survey plan showing the isolated church, Stow, Cambridgeshire.*

Stow is probably the clue. Its Saxon meaning was 'place' but often it meant 'a holy place'. The church was probably built here because of the pagan ritual significance of the site which was more important to its founders than proximity to the village.

Place names and descriptive names on Ordnance Survey maps also help with the discovery of sites. However descriptive names need to be accepted with care. Because the Ordnance Survey mark the word 'moat' near a set of ditches it does not necessarily mean that this is so. It may be other things, not least recent cattle drinking ponds. Thus at Lutton, in Northamptonshire, the rectangular arrangements of apparently formerly wet ditches, called 'moats' on Ordnance Survey maps, are nothing more than old roads or holloways which were still in use as late as 1800 according to the Enclosure Map of the parish. Certainly a proportion of 'moats' are in fact post-medieval gardens (see p. 136). The words 'field system' on Ordnance Survey maps also need to be treated with great care, for this general description is given indiscriminately to prehistoric and Roman 'Celtic' fields as well as to medieval strip lynchets.

Place names are of more value. The best example is the way the Ordnance Survey for years marked the site of the deserted medieval village of Hamilton in Leicestershire as 'Town of Hamilton' to the mystification of generations of map readers. Likewise the apparently purposeless name 'Elmington' printed across an otherwise undistinguished group of fields near Oundle in Northamptonshire (45) in fact gives the location of a long deserted village finally swept away by its monastic landlord in the early sixteenth century. Armed with the knowledge, acquired from the nineteenth-century parochial history of Clopton, in Cambridgeshire, that there was once a medieval manor called Rouses, the name Rouses Wood, given to a small copse in a remote corner of the parish, was regarded as significant. A field visit proved the existence of a small medieval moat there, no doubt the centre of Rouses Manor.[7] At the same simple level it is clear that the name Perio Mill, situated alone on the side of the River Nene in Northamptonshire, must have some connection with the lost village of Perio and indeed lies just close to the remaining earthworks.

Not all such place names are significant of course and care is needed all the time. Countless 'Manor Farms' and 'Granges' take their names from eighteenth- or nineteenth-century owners concerned with improving their social status and are not necessarily to be associated with possible medieval sites. Other names too can mislead. In Apethorpe, Northamptonshire, we have detailed records of a village called Hale in the parish, finally abandoned after the Black Death of 1348–49. The village name is preserved by the present Hale Field Farm in a remote part of Apethorpe parish and despite a distinct lack of any other evidence the lost village has been associated with this place.[8] In fact Hale village lay some distance away around another farm which goes by the unlikely name of Cheesman's Farm. Hale Field Farm is the name given to a building erected in the eighteenth century on a piece of land which was once a field belonging to Hale village. Therefore names on maps, while being potentially useful, need to be supported by other documentary and field evidence before they can be accepted.

Modern maps also assist the discovery of sites by the general patterns of modern fields, areas of woodland and streams. Thus a continuous curving modern hedge in an area otherwise divided into rectangular fields can sometimes give the clue to a medieval deer park. Other evidence such as park names may be relevant here. The occurrence of 'Park Wood', 'Park Coppice' or 'Park Farm' will help to pinpoint the area of the original medieval deer park (*20*). Once again however these observations need to be checked, not only against other documentary sources, but finally on the ground.

Groups of irregularly shaped fields, again surrounded by fields of highly geometric form, can easily be picked out on a large-scale Ordnance Survey plan. Such fields often indicate that they are much older than the surrounding ones and are thus always worth visiting on the ground. Even if they eventually produce no archaeological evidence of past occupation their very existence is usually significant in the overall history of the area and can play a part in building up the total picture of man's activities there. Ultimately, either through other documents, or from the botanical content of hedgerows, the age and purpose of such fields can be established and their function in relation to other purely archaeological habitation sites discovered. Thus the basic economic background of an archaeological site can gradually be built up.

Especially important indicators of lost medieval settlements preserved on modern maps are parish and other land boundaries. A certain amount of care has to be exercised here, for in many parts of the country parish boundaries have been radically altered in the last hundred years as a result of modern administrative changes. It is essential to check the existing boundaries of a parish against other evidence, especially older maps (see p. 102). But once the parish boundaries have been carefully checked and the pattern before the late-nineteenth-century changes established, one will usually have a layout of land units which is not only of great antiquity, but which has not been altered to a marked extent for a thousand years or more. For the parish boundaries of England are amongst the oldest, most permanent and important features of the historic landscape. Their apparent connection with the Church is misleading, for in origin they have nothing to do with ecclesiastical organisation. They were the carefully agreed and marked out boundaries around the agricultural land of each settlement or group of settlements. That is, parishes in the first place were basic economic units of land or estates, from which came all the available resources for subsistence agriculture, i.e. arable, pasture, meadow, fen, wood and waste. It was probably quite late in their history that some were taken over by the Church which found them useful units for ecclesiastical administration and finance. This is not the place to detail the origins of parishes, but it is perhaps worth noting that many parishes appear to have been established as land units or estates certainly by the early Saxon period and perhaps even before.[9]

From these old land units it is often possible to discover new medieval

45 Ordnance Survey plan showing the site of the deserted medieval village of Elmington, Northamptonshire.

settlement sites. The most obvious features to look for are projections or appendages of a parish, in which there is no existing settlement, or only a single farm. These projections are sometimes the result of the land of a decayed settlement being later incorporated into that of an existing village. There are many examples of this kind of parish boundary shape leading to the discovery of deserted villages.[10] Here one such case may be noted. The Cambridgeshire parish of Gamlingay has a curious promontory of land on the west in the centre of which is the modern Woodbury Farm (*46*). The obvious inference is that this projection was once a separate medieval land unit included in the parish of Gamlingay for ecclesiastical convenience. This can in fact be proved by other documentary sources and a ground visit shows that the remains of the hamlet of Woodbury, consisting of holloways and closes, still exist near the modern Woodbury Farm, incidentally quite invisible on all air photographs.[11]

This kind of work, and here we can look briefly at how other documentary sources are involved, can be taken even further (*47*). Again in Cambridgeshire there are a number of parishes which from their shapes appear to have been formed by the splitting up of formerly larger land units.[12] The parish of Childerley seems to have been cut out of a once much larger Lolworth parish and the existence of two known deserted villages at Childerley and the -ley ending to their names suggest that both these villages were set up in the waste of Lolworth and are secondary to Lolworth village. Subsequent growth led to the separation of their land from that of Lolworth. Immediately to the west of Childerley in Boxworth parish the existence of a medieval moated site with a fully documented history is further evidence of yet another secondary settlement which here never achieved separate parochial status. To the west again lie the parishes of Knapwell and Elsworth. Both the shape and layout of the parish boundaries as well as documentary evidence contained in Saxon land charters indicates that Knapwell is a secondary settlement of Elsworth and that the land of Knapwell parish has been cut out of a formerly much more extensive Elsworth. Other documentary evidence points to the fact that the present Knapwell Wood Farm is itself a medieval secondary settlement of Knapwell village. In view of all this evidence for secondary settlement in the area, much of which, such as the villages at Childerley and the moat at Boxworth, is now deserted, it is worth looking for more.

Nothing is visible on air photographs nor is there anything obvious on modern maps. However Elsworth Wood in the south of Elsworth parish looks promising, especially as our botanical colleagues regard it as of particular interest. Part of it contains plants such as Herb paris (*Paris quadrifolia*) and Dog's mercury (*Mercurialis perennis*) which are indicators

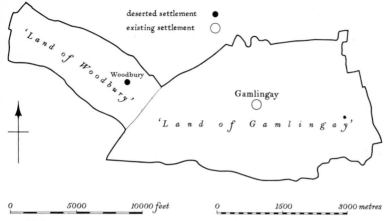

46 *Medieval settlements and estates, Gamlingay, Cambridgeshire.*

47 *Medieval settlements and estates, West Cambridgeshire.*

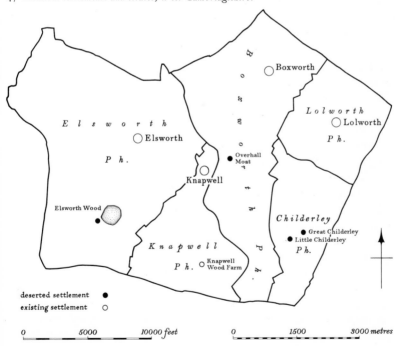

of very old and perhaps primary woodland. The Enclosure Map of 1803 shows that this wood and some fields around it were 'old enclosures' and this perhaps means that the area was never part of the common fields of the parish. In addition, in medieval documents there are various references which may belong to this place, such as Matheus *Atewode* living in the parish in 1279 and *Le Wodecroft* in the 1322 Court Roll. If we finally go to Elsworth Wood we find that around and partly within it are the earth-work remains of paddocks, closes and a holloway, all indicating the existence of a medieval farmstead. This may seem a great deal of effort to find one small medieval settlement, but it is important to note that an appreciation of the topographical history of an area can not only produce new archaeological sites, but explain much about their origins, development and even decline without excavation. In any case excavation would not give us most of this information as it is beyond the scope of the technique.[13]

The Royal Commission on Historical Monuments has used a modification of this method to discover many small medieval deserted settlements in Dorset. In the chalklands of Wessex medieval settlement was, of necessity, largely confined to the river valleys and the associated land of these settlements consequently took the form of generally rectangular strips on one or both sides of the valleys. These have often come down to us as the modern civil or ecclesiastical parishes. But even modern maps and old estate maps, where they exist, show long continuous hedgelines within the parishes running parallel to the boundaries from ridge top to valley bottom. Very often a modern parish in the chalklands can seem to have been made up from as many as ten separate land units outlined by these internal hedges. Once it is appreciated that these land units are medieval farming areas which once belonged to individual settlements, it only remains to look in the valley bottoms within these land units to find traces of the settlements.

In the valley of the North Winterbourne, in Dorset, the three modern parishes of Winterbourne Stickland, Clenston and Whitchurch can be seen to have been made up from eight of these land units, though only the villages of Stickland and Whitchurch and a scatter of isolated farms now remain. Field investigation has revealed not just the six lost settlements here but a continuous line of earthworks three and a half miles long, broken only by the existing buildings. Very little documentary work was required to identify the names of the various parts of these remains and the result was the discovery of the villages of Quarleston, Philipston (*48*), Nicholston, Whatcombe and La Lee as well as the shrunken parts of Whitchurch, Stickland and Clenston. Again in Dorset, in Charminster

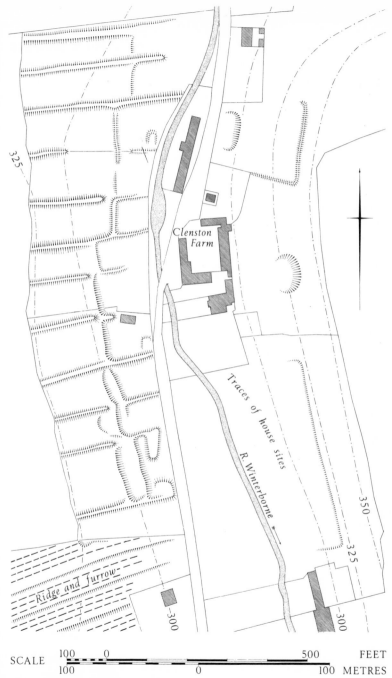

325

Clenston
Farm

Traces of house sites

R. Winterborne

350

325

300

300

Ridge and Furrow

SCALE

100   0   500   FEET

100   0   100 METRES

48 *Deserted medieval settlement of Philipston, Winterborne Clenston, Dorset.*

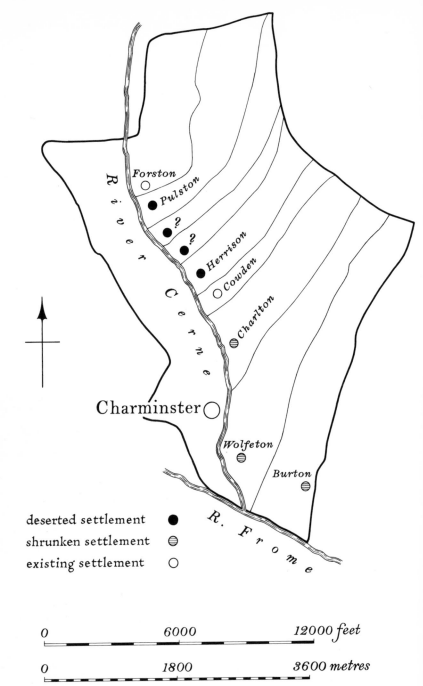

deserted settlement ●
shrunken settlement ⊜
existing settlement ○

| 0 | 6000 | 12000 feet |

| 0 | 1800 | 3600 metres |

49 *Medieval settlements and estates, Charminster, Dorset.*

parish (*49*), ten separate land units have been identified from maps, one belonging to the existing village of Charminster, five belonging to now isolated farmsteads or hamlets all of which had earthworks around them, and the other four to long deserted medieval settlements. Of these last four, documentary research has produced the names of two but the remaining two are apparently completely unrecorded in documents. Without this method of using land boundaries they would not have been looked for let alone found.[14]

Even very minor and seemingly unimportant features can be indicative of medieval sites. In Northamptonshire the site of the deserted village of Papley in Warmington parish (*50*) is recognisable on Ordnance Survey maps not by any remains of the village, which is not marked, but by the fact that four footpaths and two bridlepaths all meet at a remote and isolated corner of Warmington parish. This identification of deserted villages from converging footpaths was first used by W. G. Hoskins in Leicestershire.[15] Likewise the small closes, now destroyed but still shown

50 The deserted medieval village of Papley, Warmington, Northamptonshire
Though this appears to be a classic example of a deserted village, almost all the remaining earthworks, except for the ridge and furrow, can be proved to be of post-desertion origin.

on modern maps, on either side of a lane leading out of the village of Deenethorpe, Northamptonshire, were the clue to the discovery of an extensive area of medieval pottery and other domestic rubbish indicating that the village was once considerably larger than it is now. The closes were in fact the old gardens or crofts of the former houses.

These are just a few ways in which modern maps can be used to discover new medieval sites. There are many others, but the examples given may serve to show how important it is to use these easily available and basic sources of information.

Old maps

The next main documentary source is old maps and plans such as are usually deposited in Record Offices and other archives. Though most old maps have by now found their way into official repositories it is surprising how many others may be found in parish chests, attics and hanging on farmhouse walls. This shows only too well the need for the closest contact and good public relations in the area where work is being carried out.

The old maps which are of most value are large-scale plans of small areas, either parishes or estates. The many versions of the printed county maps of the seventeenth and eighteenth centuries are usually of limited use. Many are little more than the result of constant re-engraving or reprinting of even older maps whose accuracy is poor and whose cartographic information is limited. It may seem obvious that such maps should not be used for detailed field studies, but they often are. The writer has more than once received letters from keen local workers asking advice on the interpretation of villages that appear to have moved, or have disappeared. When questioned these workers point out that the position of the village on, say, 'Morden's Map of Essex' seems to show such a feature. This reveals an inability to realise the original function of these county maps, their standards of survey and their cartographic inaccuracies.[16]

Occasionally some of the better small-scale maps, often based on new and accurate surveys, can be useful, though they still have to be treated with care and checked against other evidence. Thomas Beighton's Map of Warwickshire of 1725 actually marks deserted villages by means of a conventional sign of an open diamond with a dot in the centre, imitating the same technique used earlier by Sir William Dugdale in his *Antiquities of Warwickshire* published in 1656.[17] A more specific example is Isaac Taylor's magnificent map of Dorset made in 1765. Today the village of More Crichel, in East Dorset, lies to the north of the church and manor house. On Taylor's map it is clearly shown south of these buildings. This suggests that the village has moved sometime subsequent to 1765 but the evidence of larger-scale plans, other documents and the inevitable field check has to be made before it can be proved that the village was indeed removed prior to landscaping in the late eighteenth century.

The strip road maps, made by Ogilby for his *Britannia* of 1675, are another sometimes useful source if one of his roads passes through the area in which one is working. In Cambridgeshire the section of the Old North Road, which Ogilby surveyed so carefully, shows a small hamlet which disappeared in the eighteenth century. Without this evidence the slight earthwork remains might never have been looked for or noted.

In the main, however, it is the large-scale Estate, Tithe and Enclosure maps and plans which are of most value and these are usually easy of access in Record Offices and Diocesan Archives. It is always worth looking at all surviving plans however obscure for they can often help. Road maps made for Turnpikes and even nineteenth-century railway construction maps all sometimes have their uses. These old maps can and should be used at first in the same way as modern Ordnance Survey maps noted above. Place names, field patterns and boundaries are all usually marked on most of these and indeed are often of more value than more recent maps for they show old hedges now removed, buildings now destroyed, or boundaries now altered.

There is however a vitally important point to be made concerning old maps. They were all made for specific purposes, usually entirely unconnected with the use to which the medieval field archaeologist is putting them. They do not necessarily show everything that existed at the time they were made, and the amount and accuracy of the detail depends on the purpose for which they were made, the interest and professional ability of the surveyor or mapmaker and sometimes the wealth, position and interests of the body or individual by whom they were commissioned. For example, one must not expect to find the remains of a deserted village shown on an eighteenth-century Enclosure map whose purpose was only to indicate cartographically the areas of land to be allotted to land owners following the enclosure of the medieval open fields. Nor is one to expect a moated site, hidden in a copse, to be depicted on a seventeenth-century estate map which was intended to show a proud owner how much arable, pasture and woodland he possessed. Even so, if one is fortunate such things are sometimes put on maps and therefore it is essential for all maps to be examined carefully, their original purpose noted and their value to the field archaeologist assessed. In a few cases, and more will certainly come to light, deserted villages are shown on old Estate maps. Professor Beresford has pointed out that a plan of Fallowfield in Northumberland, made as early as 1583, shows dotted rectangles on the site and explains them as 'old howes foundacions', and a number of other examples are also known.[18]

In many more cases old maps show houses, hamlets and even villages where nothing now exists, indicating both late desertion or removal and potential remains to be discovered. A late-eighteenth-century plan of Milton Abbas, Dorset, depicts the whole town in detail, just before it was swept away to make new parkland around the rebuilt Milton Abbas House.[19] On a much smaller and more typical level the Enclosure Map of Apethorpe in Northamptonshire, dated 1778, shows a street lined with houses to the east of the existing village. Street and houses were destroyed in the nineteenth century when the park around Apethorpe Hall was enlarged, but the map gives the clue to the still extant remains. Such examples can be multiplied many times all over the country.

Other potential sites such as moats, windmill mounds and deer parks may also be clearly marked on old maps either as already abandoned or still in use. The windmill, shown on the 1775 Enclosure Map of Dudding-

51 Part of the 1775 Enclosure Map of Duddington, Northamptonshire
The depiction of a windmill on this map gives the location and purpose of a low mound which still exists.

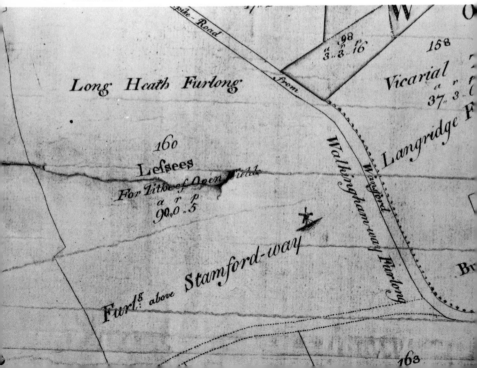

ton, Northamptonshire (51), led to the discovery of the low mound that it stood on, which might otherwise have been missed altogether on the ground.

On the other hand old maps can be deceiving. Estate maps showing the pattern of strips in the common fields, while of some value when studying ridge and furrow and other medieval cultivation remains, do not necessarily show the total area of land once cultivated in the medieval period and therefore are of little value in indicating the existence of much of the physical remains of this cultivation. Such maps obviously only show the area of arable land at the time the map was made, always some time in the post medieval period. They do not show land that was once cultivated in strips and later enclosed, or similar land later abandoned to the waste or returned to permanent pasture. Thus in Dorset, at Sutton Waldron, while a map of 1776 shows strip lynchets still being cultivated as part of the common fields of the parish, it does not mark other strip lynchets which had been abandoned by that time.[20] In this case, and in many others, only fieldwork or air photographic examination can provide evidence for the existence of such remains.

Old maps can also give information about well-known sites which is otherwise unobtainable from field examination. Even so the cartographic evidence needs to be treated with some care until it is checked, preferably by excavation. Thus the 1848 Tithe Map of Benefield, Northamptonshire, shows the circular moated enclosure known as Benefield Castle with an entrance on the east side (52). This entrance is no longer in existence and therefore the map evidence needs to be considered when interpreting the site.

Place names are particularly important on all maps, not only modern ones, and especially the names of individual fields. Estate and Tithe maps are extremely useful here for the name of each field which they often give can be of considerable antiquity and, more important, give valuable clues to the existence of medieval remains. Great care must be exercised in the interpretation of many field names for as with all place name evidence it is all too easy to jump to totally erroneous conclusions. A detailed knowledge of place names is perhaps beyond the basic needs of the medieval field archaeologist, but the relevant volumes of the English Place Name Society are reliable and useful guides as is another recent book on this subject.[21] This said, however, field names can be most useful in the discovery of sites. A number of deserted villages have been identified by the characteristic name of 'The Town' or 'Town Fields' on Estate maps. Thus the site of Kingston alias Chesterton Parva, in Warwickshire, is called 'Corne Towne' and 'Grazing Towne' on a map of 1697. Even more

52 Part of the 1848 Tithe Map of Benefield, Northamptonshire
The map shows the water-filled moat around Benefield Castle with an entrance causeway which no longer exists on the ground.

specific is a plan of East Lyton in County Durham of 1608 which actually marks 'The Scyte of the Howes'.[22]

Just as specific is the small field marked as 'site of messuage' on the 1839 Tithe Map of the village of Lastingham, in the North Riding of Yorkshire. The field was entirely filled with earthworks, which later proved to be the remains of successive buildings from the thirteenth to the late eighteenth centuries.[23]

Names such as 'Windmill Field' and 'Park Wood' and 'Park Copse' may also lead to the identification of windmill mounds and medieval deer parks. The extremely common names of 'Hall Close' or 'Hall Yard' are sometimes given to a paddock adjacent to an existing manor house or farm which has usually remained as permanent pasture and which often contains earthworks, including building platforms, fishponds and other remains associated with medieval manorial sites. A field known as Court Close, lying behind the church and manor house in Dewlish, Dorset, contains the earthwork remains of a set of rectangular paddocks, building platforms, an early moated manorial site, and a line of house sites (53),[24] while at Chelveston, Northamptonshire, a field called Water Yard on modern Ordnance Survey maps and Hall Yard on the Enclosure Map,

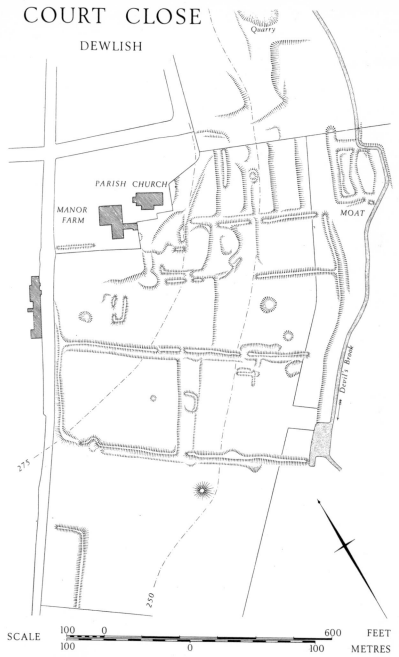

COURT CLOSE

DEWLISH

Quarry

PARISH CHURCH

MANOR
FARM

MOAT

Devil's Brook

275

250

SCALE

100   0   600   FEET

100   0   100   METRES

53 *Manorial earthworks, Court Close, Dewlish, Dorset.*

turned out to contain the earthworks of a manor house and two associated fishponds. A group of fields near Apethorpe, also in Northamptonshire, described on a map of 1778 as Old Walls and Long Walls contains the remains of the lost village of Hale.

Another very common field name is Conegar or Coneygree or variants, indicating a place where rabbits lived. Many are of no archaeological significance, but some, where during the medieval period rabbits were actually enclosed within a surrounding wall or bank, still have earthwork remains which can be discovered. The circular embanked enclosure on a hilltop at Winterbourne Stoke, Wiltshire, which surrounds a group of Bronze Age barrows is still known as the Coneygar, and was the manorial rabbit warren, whose inhabitants lived, apparently happily, by burrowing in the barrows. More unusual, but of similar interest, is the name Hare Park, in Cambridgeshire, whose recognition ultimately led to the discovery of the enclosing bank round a small area of land, constructed in the early seventeenth century for the purpose of containing hares.[25]

Field names which refer to the type of soil there when ploughed are also worth noting and ground checking. Blacklands, in an area of light-coloured soils, can result from the occurrence of occupation rubbish of a previously unrecorded medieval settlement while Chequer Field has been known to indicate the existence of the stone walls of a deserted village. Other field names known to have produced evidence of medieval sites are Mill Leaze or Mill Close, Fishponds, Crockmeads, Potgastons, Harpits and names ending in -stan or -bury.[26]

Of course field names can also indicate sites of Roman or even prehistoric origin. The field in which the remarkable and well-known Hinton St Mary mosaic, now in the British Museum, was found was called Stoney Hill on the Tithe Map of 1843, a name given to it presumably because of the vast quantities of Roman building materials ploughed up from the villa there.[27] However such discoveries must be expected. In any case these field names often turn up both medieval and earlier material together as at Pewsey, in Wiltshire, where a field called Black Patch has produced Iron Age occupation material as well as an important Anglo-Saxon cemetery.[28]

Sometimes it is necessary to delve deeper into the meaning and original form of field names to see their significance. The name Stonehurst Wood in a remote Cambridgeshire village, recorded on the Tithe Map of 1840, is seemingly of no importance. It was called by this name in 1663, but in 1315 a document records it as Stonhaus, and the remains of a small medieval farmstead were discovered here as a result of following up this name.[29] This type of work involves a knowledge of other documents, to which we must now turn.

Printed records

Before the keen archaeologist turns to original documents he should take note of the information contained in published histories of the area on which he is working. Original records either published in full or in calendar form by the Public Record Office and local and national Record Societies should also be consulted. These often contain useful information to guide him to new sites in the field without the difficulty of understanding the original documents.

The easiest to use are the old county histories, often published in the eighteenth or nineteenth centuries. These vary considerably in their value and accuracy and need to be treated with care. Many are useless when trying to find new sites, being made up largely of long descriptions of church monuments and interminable family trees of obscure people. The best however are very useful and much information can be obtained from them. In *The Antiquities of Warwickshire*, published in 1656, Sir William Dugdale noted 'depopulated places' and John Bridges in his *History and Antiquities of Northamptonshire*, written about 1720 but not published until 1791, went further. He sometimes gave long descriptions of deserted villages and more often wrote short but valuable notes on a site. Thus at the deserted village of Downton he notes that 'large foundation stones and causeys' had been found there, while at Kingsthorpe, near Polebrook, 'hollow places with marks and foundations of a village' were still visible (2).[30]

These examples are of course quite specific and the result of direct observation or contemporary knowledge. More often the information is taken from original documents and is not at all specific. In J. Nichol's *History and Antiquities of Leicestershire*, vol. I, published in 1798, there is a typical example in which the author quotes a charter of 1448 whereby King Henry VI 'granted to Thomas Palmer Esq. and his heirs, leave to enclose and empark 300 acres of land in Holt'. He gives no indication of the whereabouts of this deer park, beyond the fact that it lay in the parish of Neville Holt. It requires the examination of old and existing maps and finally fieldwork to establish the site of this deer park and to identify its boundaries. Nevertheless this kind of information at least gives the field archaeologist an idea of what existed. Likewise Nash in his *History and Antiquities of Worcestershire* (1781) quotes a Court Roll of the Manor of Warley of 1485–86, which mentions 'Le Parke Field' as part of the manor. Here again we may be able to find the site of this park, now that its existence is known.

The same kind of information is easily obtainable from the vast numbers of calendared documents and others published in full by the Public Record

Office, local Record Societies and various other organisations. Thus in the Historical Manuscripts Commissions *Report* on the documents owned by the Earl of Verulam at Gorhambury, Hertfordshire, there is a reference in a seventeenth-century survey to a 'warren of Coneys well stored and the burrows in good repair, upon 72 acres within the park'. Here is an approximate location for a type of site, which often consisted of earthworks, usually large earthen mounds built to help the rabbits burrow, which would repay the time spent in field investigation. An example of the combing of published records for reference to medieval pottery manufacturing sites has already been published and gives a good idea of the variety of documents likely to produce such information.[31]

This use of published documents is ideal for the beginner for it involves little more than factual statements of what was at a certain place in the past, which can then be discovered if the remains still exist. It avoids the more complex matters of the detailed interpretation of documents which will be dealt with later.

Original documents

The range of original written documents available to the medieval field archaeologist is truly enormous. It is virtually impossible to say what kind of document will be of most value to him when trying to discover new sites. Almost any type of document regardless of date from Saxon charters to late-nineteenth-century deeds can and sometimes does produce information. However, as we shall see, information is usually only of value when combined with evidence from many other sources. By and large a full-scale attack on all the available documents relating to a parish or a group of parishes merely to discover archaeological sites is not to be recommended. It will usually involve a great deal of work, which could be more usefully done in the field. Much better is to leave original documents to a later stage in the work when one is trying to identify the sites discovered by other methods. At that stage clues to other remains may well emerge.

The kind of information that can come from original documents varies greatly. At a very simple level one might find a reference such as that in a late-eighteenth-century deed for a Cambridgeshire village which describes a paddock as 'where a house formerly stood'. Even here, a brief reconnaissance along the village street would have already revealed that the site existed as earthworks and thus in a sense the document is giving us information about the interpretation of the site, i.e. by what date it was already abandoned, rather than actually giving us a new site.

One of the most useful sources of information, though involving certain problems of interpretation and validity, is the Saxon Land Charter. These charters give the boundaries of the land being granted to various peoples and organisations in the pre-Conquest period. They often include in their boundary points various places which existed when the charter was made, but which have either now disappeared, or are not recognisable in their present form.

Thus in four separate mid-tenth-century charters for a group of Dorset parishes, there is a reference to an Old Man's Farm (Ealdmannes Werthe or Wyrth, Eldmanmes Wrthe etc.) which can be identified as having lain close to the point where the present parish boundaries meet. There is certainly no modern farmstead in the area, nor is there any record of one in the later documents but it ought to be possible given the approximate location to discover this Saxon farmstead.[32] More specifically, in a charter of 941 for Buckland Newton one of the boundary points is a *Hawen* (Hagen), that is, probably a wooded enclosure for game. At this point in the modern boundary there is still a wood, Grange Wood, and it is still defined by a well-marked bank and ditch.[33]

That great record of late-eleventh-century England, Domesday Book, can also be of immense value in the identification of possible lost villages, but it needs to be treated with the greatest of care, and its method of compilation, purpose and vagaries fully understood.[34] By no means all settlements that existed are listed in it and any places that are recorded were not necessarily villages or even hamlets. This is especially true in the Highland Zone of Britain where the apparent normal entry for specific villages can now be seen as merely the convenient grouping together for purely administrative or tenurial purposes of what were in fact as many as 50 separate isolated and individual farmsteads.[35]

When studying Domesday Book all kinds of problems and oddities may appear. In Wiltshire, for example, Domesday Book has five separate entries for a place called Frustfield. This name only occurs in later medieval times as the name of a Hundred occupying the modern parishes of Whiteparish and Landford in the south east of the county. One might easily start looking for a lost deserted village of Frustfield given only this information. However the unravelling of the manorial history of the area would prove that this is a waste of time, for it can be shown that Frustfield was the name given to five separate settlements all of which still exist. Two of them, now grown together, are the present village of Whiteparish, and the other three are isolated farmsteads. All have very different names now and that of the main village was changed from Frustfield to Alderstone, then to Whitchurch and finally Whiteparish between 1086 and 1220.[36] This is just one instance of the kind of complications to be found in Domesday Book and the dangers therein for the archaeologist brought up to understand that written documents mean what they say. There are many others (see pp. 137–8).

Other documents too, while they can be valuable in giving general locations of sites, are sometimes dangerously misleading. The existence in the fourteenth-century Manor Court Rolls of Elsworth in Cambridgeshire of the name *Le Wodecroft* can help towards the discovery of a deserted farmstead there (see p. 98). Yet a similar record in Dorset could have led to serious errors. There in Stalbridge parish, medieval records refer to a place called *Newnham*, which is now unknown. In this particular area within a medieval forest, Newnham ought to be a medieval farmstead established in the waste of the parish and therefore one should be looking for the remains of a small deserted settlement. However no such remains exist or existed for the Tithe map of the parish for 1839 clearly identifies Newnham as a now unnamed group of barns and cowsheds.[37] This illustrates well the dangers of using the information contained in one document or class of document without finding supporting evidence from elsewhere. This fact cannot be stressed too often for it is all too easy to jump to conclusions.

Another example, also from Dorset, will confirm this. Domesday Book records the existence of a place called Colber (*Colesberie*) in the county. Later records place it within the parish of Sturminster Newton and suggest that it was a large and thriving village. For example, the 1333 Subsidy Rolls record 22 taxpayers living at Colber, which could mean a total population of perhaps a hundred, a large place by Dorset standards. As there is no record of the village of Colber after the seventeenth century one can assume that it was deserted before that date. However no large deserted village in fact exists for Colber was the name given, not to a single village, but to a large area of land which still contains at least ten farmsteads of medieval origin as well as two hamlets. When the original site of Colber was discovered, by visiting the field still known locally as 'Colbers', it proved to be the earthworks of a small isolated farmstead and its paddocks (*17*). The remains are an interesting example of a deserted medieval manor house or farm, but they are not the deserted village that the documents might lead one to expect.[38]

Finally in this section, let us look at the manner in which new sites may be discovered using a whole host of documents of various kinds, combined with fieldwork. These examples are not given as typical ones, for there is no such thing, but they do show what the medieval field archaeologist must be aware of when using documents.

The first example is a settlement known as Philipston, which, from the occurrence of its name in many records, seems to have been somewhere in the modern parish of Wimborne St Giles in Dorset. Here on the edge of the east Dorset chalklands, the modern and indeed medieval parishes were often made up of groups of settlements and their associated land units (see p. ∞ above). Here at once we see the need for a wide knowledge of medieval settlement history in the area being examined. In the parish of Wimborne St Giles there were and still are three separate villages, Wimborne St Giles itself, Wimborne All Hallows and Monkton Up Wimborne (54). At first sight it is not clear whether the alleged settlement of Philipston was an alternative name for one of these or a separate village in its own right. To be sure about this we have to trace the manorial descent of the three existing villages as well as that of Philipston. This can be a slow and laborious process, regarded by present-day local historians (often justifiably) as being of little value, but it sometimes does pay dividends in this kind of work. By studying the County History, written in the nineteenth century, and the volume on Domesday Book of the Victoria County History, we find that Philipston was held throughout the medieval period by Wilton Abbey, in Wiltshire, while none of the other villages was connected with the abbey at all. Therefore Philipston is likely to have been a separate settlement.

The next problem is to establish its location. Here again various documents help. In the 1241 Curia Regis Rolls (in the Public Record Office) there is a court case which includes details of a 'way' extending from the land of Philipston to the wood of 'Suthdun'. This wood still exists as Sutton Holmes which lies in the extreme south east of Wimborne St Giles parish and the county Place Name Survey proves this conclusively. In the De Banco Rolls for 1285 (again in the Public Record Office), there is a dispute about animals which were being driven to Philipston and which escaped into the fields of Knowlton. Knowlton, in Woodlands parish, lies due south of Wimborne St Giles parish. Therefore it is likely, though not absolutely certain, that Philipston lay somewhere in the southern part of Wimborne St Giles parish. Proof of this comes from the Tithe Map of Wimborne St Giles (1839), which not only records the names Upper and Lower Philipston Field but actually gives the name Philipston Farm to an existing house in the area.

Yet even so this is still not the site of Philipston, as an examination of the modern maps reveals. The parish of Wimborne St Giles is a curious shape. This is largely because it is made up of a series of early medieval or Saxon estates, the boundaries of which are still traceable as continuous modern hedge lines. We can therefore identify the land of Wimborne St Giles, Wimborne All Hallows and Monkton Up Wimborne as well as

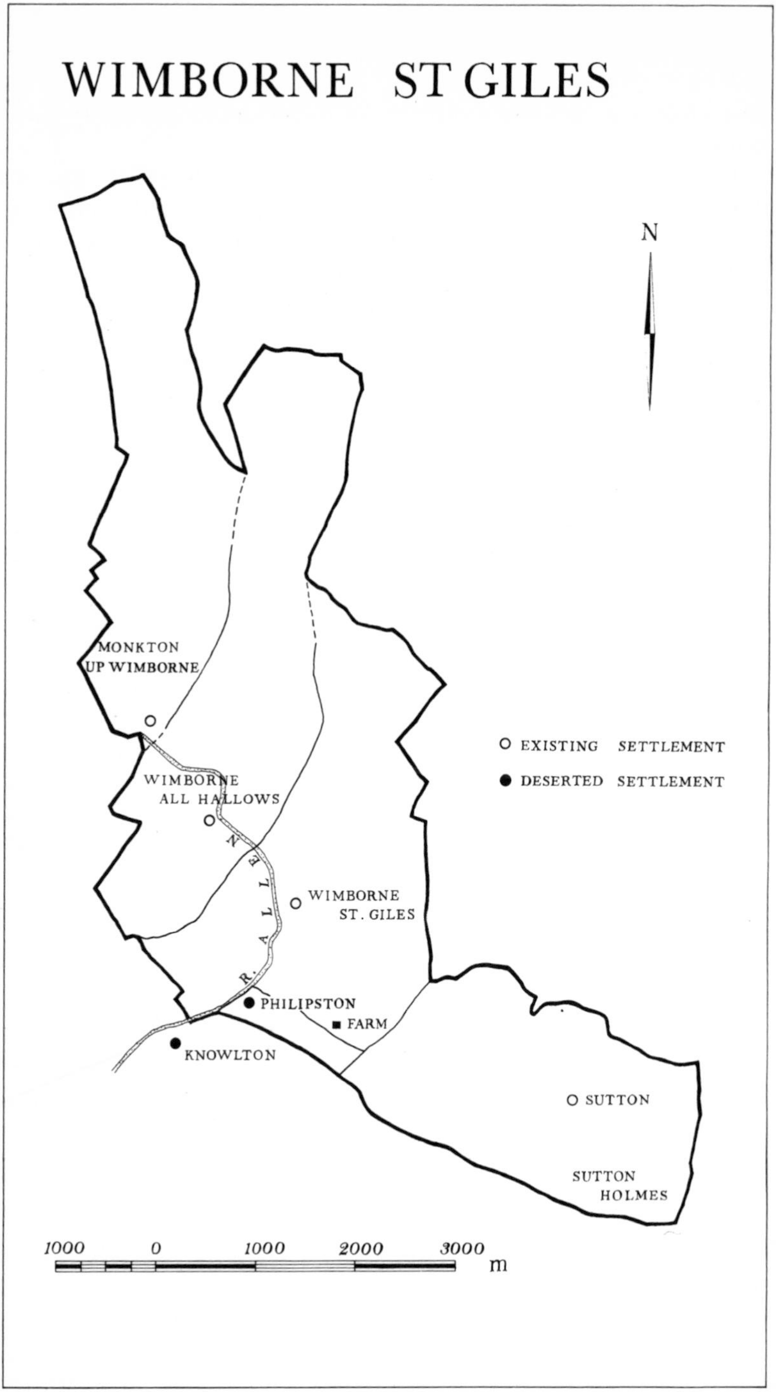

WIMBORNE ST GILES

N

○ EXISTING SETTLEMENT
● DESERTED SETTLEMENT

MONKTON
UP WIMBORNE
○

WIMBORNE
ALL HALLOWS
○

R. ALLEN

○ WIMBORNE
ST. GILES

● PHILIPSTON
■ FARM

● KNOWLTON

○ SUTTON

SUTTON
HOLMES

1000   0   1000   2000   3000 m

54 *Medieval settlements and estates, Wimborne St Giles, Dorset.*

that of another small settlement in the south east of the parish called Sutton.

In addition we can then see clearly the land of Philipston. This is a long narrow strip still bounded by continuous modern hedgelines south of the Wimborne St Giles land. While the fields named Upper and Lower Philipston Field lie within this area the farm called Philipston Farm on the Tithe Map does not. It lies on the other side of the estate boundary in the land of Wimborne St Giles. Therefore the farm cannot be the site of Philipston. In any case, by analogy with all other medieval settlements in the area, the farm set back as it is from the river would be a very unusual place for a medieval settlement. So having established the land of Philipston if we finally go out into the field and look at the low-lying ground, close to the River Allen, we immediately find the earthwork remains of Philipston.[39]

Another example is in a very different area, in Rutland, and is perhaps less complex. Here Domesday Book records the existence of a village called Snelston (Smelstone), and its name appears in a variety of later records. However it certainly no longer exists and can be regarded as a deserted medieval village. All this is conveniently listed in the Victoria County History of *Rutland*, vol. II. In an earlier volume of the V.C.H., F. M. Stenton suggested that the village must have lain near the existing village of Stoke Dry, but no trace remained of it (55). In 1954, Professor Beresford in his book, *The Lost Villages of England*, noted that there was a large area in the south of the parish of Stoke Dry completely empty of all existing settlements. He therefore suggested that Snelston may have been here. He also pointed out that in all late medieval taxation records Snelston was listed as Caldecott, an existing village south of Stoke Dry parish. Here then was the basic evidence for the supposed whereabouts of a potential deserted village site. It only remained to find it.

The workers involved with this problem first looked at Cary's Map of Rutland in 1787. This map drawn at approximately 1:25,000 marks 'Snelston Ruins' somewhere between Stoke Dry and Caldecott villages. Local enquiries in the area resulted in an least two people in Caldecott telling of the tradition that 'the old Roman village of Snelston' once lay at the north end of Caldecott parish. Knowing the approximate area of the village it was then not difficult to discover the site itself. The modern 2½-in. and 6-in. Ordnance Survey maps of Caldecott parish show as usual all the existing field hedges. These, as one expects in the East Midlands, where enclosure of the former medieval common fields was late and carried out as a result of Parliamentary Enclosure Acts, are laid out in a strictly geometrical form. All the fields have straight sides and right-angled corners except at one place in the north of the parish. Here there are three small

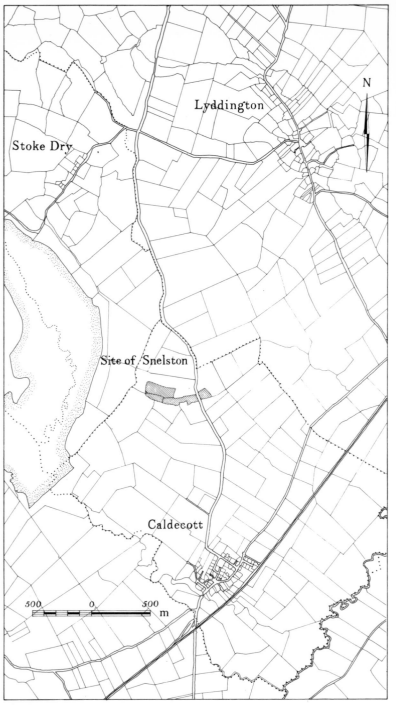

55 *Modern field pattern, Caldecott and Stoke Dry parishes, Rutland, showing the site of the deserted settlement of Snelston.*

fields of markedly irregular appearance with hedge lines which wander about and have marked bends or kinks in them. These fields, by their very form, look as if they are much older than the surrounding ones. This then seemed to be the most likely site for the village of Snelston, and so it proved to be. Within these fields exists a well-marked holloway with small paddocks bounded by earthen banks on either side of it, and a number of building platforms. It only remained to make an accurate plan of the earthworks and the work of recording was completed.[40]

For the final example of this work of complex discovery, we can move south again to Northamptonshire, to the parish of Gretton. Here the valuable book on *The Deserted Villages of Northamptonshire* (1966), by K. J. Allison et al., records the existence of a place called *Cotes* or *Coten*. The name alone suggests that this was no village but only a small hamlet or single farm, and the medieval records quoted in the book support this. in 1290 the manor of Cotes consisted of only one messuage or farmstead and 80 acres of land, while in 1355 there were still only one messuage and 200 acres of land. The county historian, writing in 1720, claimed there was still one house at Cotes, but today nothing remains and the whereabouts of the site was for a time unknown. The authors of the book on the deserted villages of Northamptonshire suggested that as the modern Ordnance Survey maps marked a number of wells on a steep slope in the south west of the parish this might be the site, but there was no other proof.

Then a group of students led by a competent field archaeologist started work on the problem. A map dated 1615 of the area came to light in the archives of nearby Rockingham Castle. This showed clearly that the large fields, which still exist in the west of Gretton parish along the Rockingham parish boundary, were at that time all known as Cotes Field, or Cotten Meadow. As the whole area was under permanent arable and no upstanding earthworks were to be expected, a field walking expedition was organised and all these large fields were systematically combed by the students. Disappointingly nothing whatever was found. The walking revealed the existence of long low ridges running across these fields, which were correctly interpreted as the remains of the headlands of the former common fields, thus showing that the area was part of the medieval arable land of the parish, therefore village remains were unlikely to be found.

Then the seventeenth-century map was examined yet again and it was noticed that in a corner of it, badly damaged by wear, and hardly visible at first sight, were a series of very small paddocks, all called Cotten Closes. These paddocks have long since been destroyed and incorporated into another large modern arable field. This area seemed more promising and was therefore visited. Immediately medieval pottery and stone rubble were picked up and then the very slight remains of earthworks in the last stages of destruction were noticed. These were quickly surveyed and the areas of pottery and rubble plotted. The resulting plan showed clearly the existence of a small farmstead consisting of a number of building sites arranged around a central yard. Only one problem remained. All the pottery found was of medieval date, except for enough Romano-British material to indicate earlier occupation of the site. But where was the single house recorded in 1720? Continued walking showed that this lay only 50 yards away, though on the other side of the modern road. Here more earthworks, almost totally destroyed by ploughing, were covered with eighteenth-century pottery, bricks and tiles. Cotes and much of its history had been found.

These are some examples of the way in which the totality of documentary evidence can be used together with fieldwork to discover new medieval settlements. It is not always as difficult as this, but having finished his task the archaeologist will not only have discovered a new site, but he should have learnt a great deal about the use and value of documents. He should also have established an understanding of the total pattern of medieval settlement in his area, which will stand him in good stead for further work.

Though this book is largely concerned with work on medieval sites in rural areas, it is worth pointing out that there is also much to be done on medieval sites in urban areas. This work falls into two distinct categories.

There is the normal archaeological fieldwork, often to be combined with excavation, which involves the watching of all building and redevelopment activities in towns. Much information is being lost all the time through urban development and renewal, especially when old buildings with shallow foundations are replaced by modern structures with deep basements. Of course not all the finds will be medieval and remains of all periods are likely to be encountered. The value of recording medieval finds from a town, albeit over many years, may be seen in Cambridge. Here, with the help of documentary research, the distribution and date of pottery and other material, carefully noted and recorded over a period of more than a century, has enabled workers to postulate exactly how the town expanded from its original nucleus over the centuries.[41]

A more specialised form of research is the recording of normal medieval sites now utterly destroyed by later urban expansion. Very little of this kind of work has as yet been carried out, though a fine example has been published for London.[42] The research involves the examination of Estate, Tithe and Enclosure maps in order to identify former moats, house sites and deer parks as well as other records which mention and give the history of such remains.

6 Interpretation of sites by documents

The use of documentary sources to interpret a medieval or later archaeo-logical site can be both relatively simple and extremely complex. Basically documents can be used to do three things. Firstly they can be used simply to tell us what a site is, secondly they can tell us what it consisted of when it was occupied or used. Finally they can help to give us the history of a site. Sometimes documents can give us the answers we require just by themselves but, as with the discovery of sites, more often they are only one source of information which has to be combined with fieldwork to obtain the full story.

At the simplest level, that is explaining exactly what a site is, documents in the form of easily accessible and understandable maps can be used in the same way as that described in the previous chapter. Thus a circular mound, discovered on the ground or from air photographs, can be proved to have been the site of a post-windmill if an old estate map depicts a windmill there (57). If however, as often happens, there is ridge and furrow associated with the mound, field interpretation is necessary to decide whether the mound lies on the ridge and furrow or is respected by it, or indeed is later than it. This kind of information is unlikely to come from documents. A mound at Wadenhoe, Northamptonshire, known to have been the site of a medieval windmill, can be shown by field examination to have been erected on uncultivated ground. The surrounding land was then ploughed into ridge and furrow. Subsequently the mill was abandoned and ploughing was then extended onto the mound, resulting in a marked alteration of its original form.

Sometimes even the simplest documentary check can avoid serious mis-takes. In the parish of Stapleford, near Salisbury in Wiltshire, there is a trapezoidal enclosure bounded by a low bank and external ditch. It was given the name South Kite by O. G. S. Crawford because of its shape and it was interpreted as either a Roman or prehistoric pastoral enclosure. More recently it was excavated by a university Department of Archaeology with no result whatsoever except to prove that it lay over 'Celtic' fields, a fact that could be ascertained by field observation alone. However the

Tithe Map of Stapleford of 1848 shows that the enclosure was then called The Conegar, which is exactly what it is, a medieval rabbit enclosure.[1]

A rather different example, but also illustrating how useful documentary checking can be, is a site at Longstowe, in Cambridgeshire. Here in the grounds of a manor house, fieldwork led to the discovery of a medieval moat, with a rectangular island of about 0·25 hectare, completely surrounded by a wide water-filled ditch. This appeared to be a perfect example of the commonly occurring pattern of an abandoned moat with an existing manor house nearby. However the 1799 Enclosure Map of the parish showed that the site was occupied by a hexagonal pond and other ditches, apparently part of a seventeenth-century garden. The 'moat' therefore is an early-nineteenth-century garden feature.[2]

Another example is the so-called Castle at Higham Ferrers, in Northamptonshire. Here the remains consist of a massive and deep L-shaped pond, with a large mound, apparently of spoil, along the side of it. It has always been interpreted as the remains of Higham Ferrers Castle, but its true function is easily explained by reference to a map of Higham Ferrers parish made in 1798, where it is marked as Coney Garth. The original castle site, some distance away and now entirely built over, is called Castle Yard (56). Indeed the castle mound itself is shown on an earlier map of 1591 within the Castle Yard.[3] The pond therefore is no more than a medieval fishpond, while the 'spoil heap' is the actual mound in which the rabbits were kept, the whole being an example of manorial food supply. Further details of the rabbit warren and fishpond are fully published in an account of the fourteenth-century Manor Court Rolls of Higham Ferrers.[4]

This kind of identification can also help ascertain the origin of the host of smaller non-archaeological sites which can sometimes cause confusion, such as shallow quarrying, copse banks, and drinking ponds for stock. All these are often shown in their original form and named on old Ordnance Survey maps as well as on Tithe, Enclosure and Estate maps. Thus the small rectangular depression within the shrunken village of Luddington, in Northamptonshire, which looks like a former house site, is shown as a pond on the Enclosure Map of 1808. It has since been filled in and grassed over. Likewise the uneven earthworks on the fen edge near Lode, in Cambridgeshire, which seem at first sight to be the remains of a settlement of some antiquity, are shown on an early nineteenth-century map as brick-pits, still being dug for clay in the 1820s.

Even modern maps can prevent the most dreadful mistakes being made in the interpretation of earthworks. A low rectangular platform, set inside a neat earthen boundary bank in a Northamptonshire valley, has been

56 Part of a 1796 Estate Map of Higham Ferrers, Northamptonshire
The map shows a large L-shaped pond which still exists and which is said to be the remains of the moat round the medieval castle. In fact the pond bounds the enclosed rabbit warren (Coney Garth) and the actual site of the castle is indicated by the name Castle Yard further to the south.

described in print as a medieval watermill site. However the 1900 edition of the Ordnance Survey 6-in. plan shows it as the clubhouse of a golf course, set in a large garden!

These examples show how it is possible to determine the purpose of a site at one moment in time and to some extent interpret the remains that still exist. In other cases the actual identification of a particular settlement is possible from maps. There is in the parish of Piddlehinton, Dorset, a large group of earthworks clearly marked on Ordnance Survey maps and obviously the remains of a deserted village (57). The modern farm there is called Little Piddle Farm and Little Puddle Village is recorded in numerous documents, many easily accessible in the County History. It would be easy and justifiable to assume therefore that all the existing remains are those of the former village of Little Puddle, but the situation is more complicated. Other documents record a place called Combe Deveral, obviously very close to Little Puddle and usually listed with it. A county historian writing in the nineteenth century suggested, quite reasonably, that it was an alias of Little Puddle, a common occurrence in that part of the world. Closer examination points to the fact that Little Puddle and Combe Deveral were separate settlements each with a different tenurial history. Yet we have only one group of earthworks.

The explanation of this situation comes from the 1842 Tithe Map of Puddletown which shows that the present parish boundary between Piddlehinton and Puddletown to the south of the earthworks is a recent alteration and that up to the late nineteenth century the parish boundary actually passed through the centre of the remains. While therefore the earthworks on the south side of the old parish boundary, where Little Piddle Farm stands, must be the remains of Little Puddle Village, those north of the old parish boundary cannot be as they lay in a different parish. The identification of these is confirmed by the names given to fields adjacent to them on the Piddlehinton Tithe Map of 1840 which records them as Deverals Mead and Deverals Bottom. This part of the earthworks is therefore the village of Combe Deveral.

The identification of the two separate villages out of one apparently single group of earthworks has other implications. It also affects the interpretation of the documented history of the site. We have figures giving the population of Little Puddle at various times in the medieval period and it is relevant to know that these refer to two villages. This is turn affects our interpretation of the density of population in Little Puddle Village and the number of possible house sites. Incidentally we have no population figures for Combe Deveral and these must be included within the totals for the existing Piddlehinton Village, another reason why Combe Deveral has to be identified. By similar means two other settlements in the same area have also been named.[5]

In the previous chapter we showed how Estate and Tithe maps could aid the discovery of cultivation remains. They can also help in interpretation. The existence of a map showing the open fields of a parish before enclosure

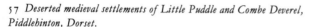

57 *Deserted medieval settlements of Little Puddle and Combe Deverel, Piddlehinton, Dorset.*

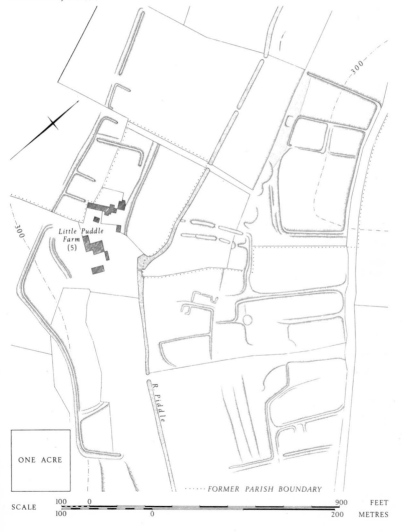

enables the detailed relationships between ridge and furrow or strip lynchets and the land holdings *at the time the map was made* to be understood.
This latter point is fundamental for, as we noted earlier, there is clear
evidence of massive and constant alteration of medieval field systems both
in terms of physical remains and in tenurial organisation.[6] Usually what
remains on the ground as ridge and furrow or strip lynchets agrees with the
general arrangements of strips and furlongs shown on open field maps.
Thus the existence of unusually wide ridges, up to 12m. across in Lolworth,
in Cambridgeshire, can be correlated exactly with the arrangement of
strips shown on the 1842 Tithe Map of the parish. The abnormal width is
the result of an individual farmer ploughing his land in a slightly different
way from that of his neighbours holding the adjacent strips. The map
certainly tells us nothing of the pre-mid-nineteenth-century picture and it
is dangerous to imply that this situation had always existed.[7] Anyone who
studies the vagaries of ridge and furrow will quickly become aware of the
field evidence and it is field evidence alone that tells of constant adaptation
and alteration due to changes in ploughing techniques.

At Turnworth, in Dorset, close examination of narrow ridge and furrow
only 3 m. across shows this to be the result of splitting former 7-metre-
wide ridges in two by later ploughing.[8] Likewise at Newport Pagnell, in
Buckinghamshire, a whole block of 8-metre-wide ridge and furrow suddenly turns into narrow 3-metre-wide ridges half way along its length.

Often fieldwork on agricultural remains is useful in explaining what is
shown on open field maps rather than *vice versa*. The sterile academic argu-
ment of some years ago on the existence or non-existence of baulks or
divisions between strips in the medieval open fields, which rages through
the pages of the *Agricultural History Review*, was notable for the lack of field
evidence by the various contributors.[9] There are indeed examples of
curious flat, unridged strips, bounded by upstanding low banks or baulks,
though these are rare and need to be clearly distinguished from long
(Roman) 'Celtic' fields.[10] More often, the term 'baulk', referring to un-
ploughed strips in arable fields shown on old maps, can easily be explained
by detailed ground examination. For example on a fine map of Wimpole,
in Cambridgeshire, of 1638, a group of 'baulks' are marked. These, as a
result of seventeenth- and eighteenth-century emparking, which has
preserved the area intact, can be identified on the ground. The baulks are in
fact normal ridges which were merely out of cultivation when the map was
made and are quite indistinguishable from the adjacent ridges.[11]

Similarly the fine map of the medieval fields of Padbury, Buckinghamshire, made in 1591, shows all the then existing strips in detail giving their
acreages and owners. It also shows uncultivated blocks of land within the

strips. On the ground or from air photographs it is possible to identify these blocks and correlate them with damp or marshy ground that, in the sixteenth century and later, it was not worth cultivating. However field-work also shows the existence of battered and worn-down ridges in some of these areas, their ends truncated by the later ridge and furrow which can be correlated with the strips on the map. These old ridges show that some time before the late sixteenth century, perhaps in the early fourteenth century when there was land hunger, these marshy areas were in fact cultivated. This fact neither the map nor any other documents will tell us.

The same map also shows a typical broad green lane, called Whadden Waye, leading between two of the large open fields. Air photographs and ground examination show this way as a raised headland with normal ridge and furrow on either side. This agrees with the map. But in addition there are slight traces of ridge and furrow on the headland itself which indicate that at some time earlier than the sixteenth century it had been necessary to overplough this headland.[12]

So far we have been concerned with the interpretation of archaeological sites entirely in terms of the information obtainable from various types of maps. It is now time to look at the use of other written records for this purpose.

The variety of documents, in the strictest sense, which the medieval field archaeologist can use is quite bewildering and the beginner can be forgiven if he concludes that he cannot possibly cope with them. They include everything from Anglo-Saxon charters, through national and local medieval records, written in seemingly unreadable Latin, to post-medieval leases, minute books and terriers, often couched in cumbersome legal terminology even when fairly easy to read. Yet while only a small propor-tion of these documents will provide useful information for the field archaeologist, any type can and often does produce a useful piece of knowledge.

How much documentary work can or needs to be done depends on the type of remains, and more important the survival of the documentary record, as well as the ability or keenness of the fieldworker in delving into and trying to understand often complex documents. In a sense the docu-mentary background for the total history is the least necessary part of the work. Short of a major disaster the documents which refer to the sites will still be available for the next generation of archaeologists and historians to study. The sites probably will not. Therefore having found, recorded or interpreted a site by the methods described so far, the archaeologist may feel that he has done enough. Yet some people, after having carried out such work, still desire to deal with the historical side and so present a reasonably complete picture. This sometimes means tackling rather detailed documentary interpretation but as much information comes from the field-work as from the documents and the two must always go hand in hand.

Here we will look briefly at some of the simpler and more obvious sources of information which the field archaeologist can make use of if he so wishes, with examples of the type of evidence contained therein. Basically there are two types of documents, those in the National Archives, such as the Public Record Office and the British Museum, and those in the Local Record Offices and Diocesan Archives.

By far the best sources of information, at least to begin with, are the various surveys, accounts and inquisitions in the Public Record Office in London. The lists of documents in the printed Indexes to *Rentals and Surveys*[13] and *Accounts*[14] as well as the typescript indexes in the Public Record Office are the usual starting places, for the documents they list often give information about physical features which have an economic value. The same economic interest by the medieval administrative machinery led to the enormous group of documents resulting from enquiries by the Crown into the value of the possessions of its tenants-in-chief and even sometimes the sub-tenants. Amongst the most useful of these are the *Inquisitions Post Mortem*, many of which are published in calendar form.[15] Particularly valuable are the detailed *extents* or descriptions which often indicate the presence and character of various buildings on a site. However these are rarely published in full and it is usually necessary to go back to the original documents. Another class of documents is the *Inquisitions Ad Quod Damnum*[16] which were enquiries to discover what loss to the Crown would result from changes and alterations proposed by its subjects. These proposals include the erection of new buildings, construction of new roads and bridges and the creation of parks. Much similar information is also listed in a less detailed form in the *Calendars of Charter Rolls, Patent Rolls, Fine Rolls*, and especially the *Calendars of Inquisitions Miscellaneous*.[17]

The kind of information contained in these documents may be illustrated by two examples. The first is the circular moated site, called Burgh Hall, at Tuttington in Norfolk, which is known to have been a medieval Royal Hunting Lodge. In an *Inquisition Miscellaneous* of 1313[19] the site is described in detail as a result of the need for £200 to be spent on repairs to it. It was then said to comprise a great hall, a chamber adjoining the hall, a chamber for the Queen, chapels, a chamber for the knights, a kitchen, a larder, two watch towers, stables, dairies, 'beast houses', bake house, brew house etc. A park enclosed by a paling, two bridges across the moat and the water-mill are also listed as well as 'the walls made of earth round the manor', which were 'in bad condition'. Here we have a detailed description that can certainly help the interpretation of many of the existing earthworks on the site.

Likewise the moated site at Newton Bromshold, Northamptonshire, which was the site of the Warrener's Lodge of the Higham Ferrers deer park, is described in a fifteenth-century Inquisition as enclosing a hall, chapel, chamber, kitchen and brew house with a dovecot and two fishponds in the grounds outside.[20] Here, though the interior of the moat is now featureless, the fishponds still survive. However their present form, due to later alterations, makes it impossible to be sure that they were originally fishponds and only the document proves it.

There are many other types of document in the Public Record Office which can be extremely useful, some of which will be mentioned later in dealing with specific examples. Much other material may be found in places such as the British Museum. Most of this is not catalogued in a published form, but at least the two volumes of the *Index to the Charters and Rolls in the British Museum* (1965 and 1967) are worth checking. Again it is quite impossible to give an idea of the totality of information that the field archaeologist can make use of. One example must suffice. In the parish of Great Wilbraham, in Cambridgeshire, air photographs taken of the former downland there show a small rectangular enclosure visible as a crop mark. It might be interpreted as either a prehistoric or a Roman settlement, but field walking has produced small quantities of medieval pottery. It can with reasonable certainty be identified as the sheepfold recorded in a survey of an estate dated 1425 as lying on 'le heth' and described as being in need of repair. This survey is one of hundreds in the Cotton Manuscripts in the British Museum.

Other valuable repositories of important documents are the archives of perpetual institutions, such as colleges and ecclesiastical organisations. These institutions had a continuing interest in land, often over many centuries, and important details of archaeological sites can be traced back in time. Thus in the archives of Pembroke College, Cambridge, a lease dated 1811 refers to a piece of pasture covering three acres, in the hamlet of Barway, which was called 'the site of the manor'. This can be identified on the ground as a small paddock still containing low earthworks including some building platforms. But the same three-acre pasture is recorded in two earlier leases of 1721 and 1649 with the same name, while finally another lease dating from 1567 was already referring to this land in the same way. Here then we have been able to track down the abandonment of this particular site to some time before the late sixteenth century.

Also in Cambridgeshire, a small close containing low earthworks in the hamlet of Long Meadow, near Bottisham, can be identified as that described in a release of 1719–20 as '1 acre of pasture in which a messuage lately stood'. This document is in the Ely Diocesan Archives.

The most obvious source of documentary information however for most medieval field archaeologists will be in their local Record Office. Once again much laborious work on a host of documents is involved in order to discover particulars of the specific sites that have been found. Before plunging into this extensive and varied material the student ought to try to understand the form, content and value of at least the main classes of documents. Some help in this sphere may be gained by looking at the very useful series of *Short Guides to Records*, published regularly over many years in the journal *History*, while F. H. Emmison's work on *Archives and Local History* (1966), and J. W. West's *Village Records* (1962), can be recommended. There are a number of other useful works which can be consulted for example, for medieval taxation records, M. W. Beresford's *Lay Subsidies and Poll Taxes* (1963) is a useful introduction.

However in the end there is no substitute for the long and often heartbreaking searches through countless records in order to find a small piece of information to interpret with certainty an individual site. Thus the field of ridge and furrow at Stanbridge in Bedfordshire, which has a small circular mound in one corner, is described in a conveyance of 1678 as 'all that pasture upon which a windmill lately stood'.[21]

Similarly at Quy, in Cambridgeshire, there is a curiously elongated island surrounded by a wide water-filled ditch, set in a broad water course, which is marked as 'moat' on Ordnance Survey maps. Fieldwork showed clearly that it could never have been a medieval moat, but it was not until a conveyance, dated 1726, in the Cambridge Record Office was seen that its origin became clear. There the site was described as having 'a gate-house over the river where the corn-mill formerly stood'. That is the 'moat' was only the old mill pond.

The detailed understanding of ridge and furrow, strip lynchets and other agricultural remains in areas where estate maps do not survive can be achieved by examining land terriers, charters, surveys and wills, all of which survive in profusion in most record offices. Yet other information on the same subject can come from the most unexpected sources. In Dorset the details of seventeenth-century enclosure of the open fields of Burton Bradstock are contained in the Church Warden's Accounts of the adjacent parish, where they record that there was no need to perambulate the parish boundaries there as they were now fixed by the new enclosures.

For some of the larger, more complex sites often the only way of finally revealing the details of their history is to rely entirely on local records. The history and decline of the now deserted village of Kingsthorpe, in

Northamptonshire (2), is barely mentioned in the national archives, because it was always included in medieval and later government records together with two other surviving villages. But 38 medieval charters, recording land transactions between peasants, a fourteenth-century terrier and a set of fourteenth-century Court Rolls, all in the Northamptonshire Record Office, enable us to trace its story. Only a small community in the late eleventh century, it remained a modest settlement until the late fourteenth century when slow decline set in.

So far we have concentrated on what a specific document or class of document can tell us about a particular site. But in the majority of cases no one record will explain everything, nor will documents alone solve our problems. It is the combination of detailed fieldwork and careful documentary research on a wide range of records which often finally explains sites. In the rest of this chapter we will examine the way in which such a combination can produce the desired result.

In the north-west of the parish of Lyddington, in Rutland, is a farm called Lyddington Park Lodge which can be noted as indicating a possible medieval deer park. Though the existing fields over most of the parish are of rigidly geometrical form, those in the area of Park Lodge are very irregular and even a cursory glance at the Ordnance Survey $2\frac{1}{2}$- or 6-in. maps shows a continuous curving boundary enclosing these fields, which cover about 100 hectares. Fieldwork not only reveals the remains of a large bank on this curving line, but also a subsidiary bank, now followed by a modern hedge and much broken down, cutting off a corner of the area. Thus fieldwork establishes the undoubted existence of a deer park here which is confirmed by Saxton's 1576 Map of Rutland, which depicts the park. Moving on to the history of this park we become involved in checking various documents. In the published *Calendar of Charter Rolls* we find that the park was first enclosed by the Bishop of Lincoln during the reign of King John. Then from other published Charter Rolls and the *Calendar of Close Rolls* we know that Henry III confirmed the original licence to enclose the park. We also have records of permission to create deer leaps in the boundary of the park (to enable deer to enter the park but not to get out) again in Henry III's reign. These are described in a Historical Manuscripts Commission *Report*, and in the Bishop's Registers, conveniently published for us by the Lincoln Record Society. At the end of the thirteenth century, the *Calendar of Patent Rolls* tells us that Edward I stocked the park with deer and that there was also a disturbance in 1291 when deer were stolen from it. Finally a Patent Roll of 1332 states that the Bishop of Lincoln's park was enlarged by 60 acres and enclosed by a stone wall in place of the old fence and hedge. Here we not only have a description of what it was like but an indication of the enlargement which agrees with the fieldwork evidence of an earlier boundary inside the existing one. In this way all the recoverable history of the site can gradually emerge.

A very different site, in which the same combination of fieldwork and documents can explain a complex development sequence, is at Fothering-hay Castle, in Northamptonshire. The castle's main contribution to popular history is as the place where Mary Queen of Scots was executed in 1587. The only obvious remains to be seen on the site are an apparently simple motte and bailey castle of typical eleventh-century form. However the competent fieldworker can not only find much more, but, with the aid of easily available documentary sources, can explain the discoveries in detail.

The motte and bailey, that comprise the castle today, were, so the *V.C.H. Northamptonshire* tells us, probably built by Simon de St Liz, Earl of Huntingdon, soon after the Norman Conquest. From then until the late fourteenth century it had a largely undistinguished history. The earliest description of the castle is dated 1341 (in an Inquisition Post Mortem) and indicates that by then only the motte, capped with a stone tower, and the bailey as we see it today existed. Within the bailey were two chapels, a great hall, chambers, and a kitchen with a gatehouse over the drawbridge. The castle was considerably rebuilt and enlarged by Edmund Langley, son of Edward III, in the late fourteenth century as the *V.C.H.* notes in detail. The work done there was not recorded but a later description, made in 1586 just before Mary Queen of Scots was sent there (given in the *V.C.H.*), mentions not only the bailey but an outer moat. Most of this outer moat still remains, though it is not shown on any map. Even the part which no longer exists is explained by a reference in the late-nineteenth-century *Northamptonshire Notes and Queries*, which tells us that it was being filled in at that time. Almost certainly this outer moat was the work of Edmund Langley. The last and most detailed description of the castle published in the parochial history is of 1625, just before its buildings were totally demolished. Here the two moats are described, and all the buildings within them were listed. If the field archaeologist makes a plan of the site, especially of the inner bailey which shows the now almost imperceptible outlines of former buildings, and correlates his work with this early-seventeenth-century description, it is possible to identify the sites of each building. Thus the chapel, chambers, great hall, kitchen, brew house, bake house, etc., can all be identified on the ground. For those with romantic interests, one can actually pinpoint within two or three metres the spot where Mary Queen of Scots was executed. Here not only can the documentary history of the site be enhanced, but future excavations greatly assisted.

This use of fieldwork and documents together to explain the site fully is nowhere better seen than at the curious Burwell Castle in Cambridgeshire. Small-scale selective excavation too has played its part in the final unravelling of a complete collection of earthworks (58). The main part of the site consists of a large rectangular 'island' which is extremely uneven and apparently broken down, completely surrounded by a massive dry ditch or moat whose bottom too is uneven. The whole is dominated by large irregular mounds up to 3 m. high lying along two sides of the moat. The documented history of the site is remarkably good. We know it was built in 1143 by King Stephen, as one of a series of castles ringing the fenlands in order to prevent the devastating raids of Geoffrey de Mandeville, then in revolt against the Crown. We also have an account written by a monk of an attack on the castle by de Mandeville in which he was killed, thus bringing about the end of the rebellion and the abandonment of the castle. However the documents do not explain the curious nature of the remains, which are not only very unlike normal twelfth-century fortifications but are also

58 Burwell Castle, Cambridgeshire
The unfinished castle with its uneven island and surrounding spoil heaps is a relic of the mid-twelfth-century Civil War. The remains of earlier gardens and house sites can be seen disappearing under the spoil heaps.

totally undefendable in any real sense. Careful fieldwork, combined with limited excavations, carried out by Lethbridge in the 1930s, proved conclusively that the castle was still being built when de Mandeville attacked it. The uneven appearance of the island results from its being covered with piles of earth prior to the erection of a high raised mound on it. The moat's present appearance is due to the fact that it was only partly dug out when construction work stopped, while the earthen mounds round it are spoil heaps composed of soil from the moat and these still retain evidence of tipping.

However Lethbridge did find late-eleventh- and early-twelfth-century pottery on the old ground surface under the central island which he could not account for. More recent fieldwork by the Royal Commission on Historical Monuments has resulted in the recognition of embanked and ditched 'crofts' partly underlain by the spoil heaps or cut by the moat, earthworks of a medieval 'long house' and part of a street or holloway, also cut by the moat. This shows that far from being built on an empty site, part of the village of Burwell was actually cleared to make way for the castle and explains the pottery found, which presumably came from the destroyed houses. Here excavation, fieldwork and documentary research have combined to elucidate the history of one particular site in a way that does not, by any means, always happen.[22]

Another example of this kind of work was that done on the so-called 'Wuduburgh' enclosure at Broad Chalke, Wiltshire (59). The small rectangular embanked enclosure, one of many on the Wessex Downlands, was excavated many years ago, and confidently assigned to the Roman period from the Romano-British pottery found in its ditches. This dating was seemingly confirmed by two Saxon land charters of AD 793–6 and 955, both of which apparently recorded the existence of the enclosure which they named as 'Wuduburgh'. This led to the inclusion of the site in a list of presumed late-Roman pastoral enclosures which formed the basic evidence for late-Roman sheep farming in Wessex. Detailed observation however showed that not only did the enclosure lie on top of medieval or later ridge and furrow, but that the ridge and furrow itself overlay earlier 'Celtic' fields. Therefore on field evidence alone the enclosure could not be Roman but must be medieval or later, though still possibly only a sheepfold. The pottery found in the ditches is derived from the earlier 'Celtic' fields, carried out onto the hillside in manure by Roman farmers.

But what of the evidence of the Saxon Charters? A careful re-analysis of these charters (fully published) showed that they had been misinterpreted, probably as a result of relying on the archaeological 'proof' and that 'Wuduburgh' actually lay some distance away on another hillside.[23] The

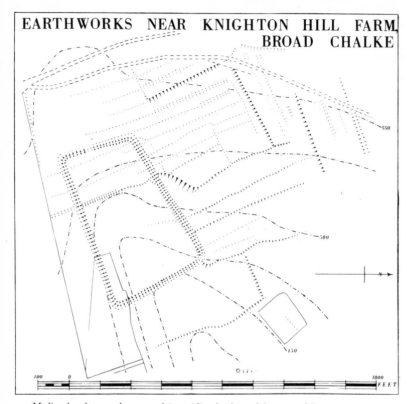

EARTHWORKS NEAR KNIGHTON HILL FARM, BROAD CHALKE

59 *Medieval or later enclosure overlying medieval ridge and furrow and Roman 'Celtic' fields, Broad Chalke, Wiltshire.*

evidence of fieldwork was thus confirmed and the way was then clear to demolish the rest of the alleged evidence, equally wrong, for late-Roman pastoral enclosures in Wessex.[24]

Back in Cambridgeshire the complications of another type of earthwork were explained by a totally different form of document. This earthwork is the great Dark Age Devil's Dyke which spans some seven miles of chalk downland and blocks the ancient Icknield Way. There is no doubt that when it was originally built it was an unbroken massive rampart and ditch. However when it was finally abandoned, gaps were cut through it to allow the passage of traffic. These can all be recognised and most of them explained. One is for the main London to Norwich Road, two are for nineteenth-century railways, one dates from the seventeenth century when Newmarket Race Course was laid out and others are the result of medieval trackways crossing it. But three of the latter, on Newmarket Heath, are extremely odd (60). In each case the rampart is broken by a ten to fifteen metre wide gap, but instead of the usual opening there is a low earthen bank closing the gap, with a small one metre wide access through the centre. The spoil from the original rampart has obviously been thrown forward into the ditch to make access through the gaps possible, but this filling has in turn been over-lain by narrow earthen causeways leading to the small holes in the low blocking bank. When these additions were first recognised they were seen as later blockings to earlier gaps through the dyke, but no date or explanation could be given for them and no obvious documents provided a clue.

The answer emerged only by accident much later when work on an entirely different and non-archaeological field was being undertaken nearby. This work was on eighteenth-century Turnpike roads and in the course of this the contemporary minute books of the Newmarket Heath Turnpike Trust were examined. Here all was made clear. Prior to the eighteenth century, traffic moving across the heath on unmade roads crossed the dyke by means of a host of gaps including the ones under discussion. When the Turnpike road was made it passed through the dyke at the largest gap and a Toll House was erected there to collect dues. However, to avoid paying these dues, travellers approaching the Toll House merely swung off the road, crossed the heath, went through the old gaps and returned to the road. The Turnpike Commissioners, obviously concerned over the loss of revenue, then blocked these gaps with the low banks that survive today. However there was an immediate outcry from the Jockey Club at this action. The Club claimed that this blocking was illegal and prevented people from moving from one racecourse to another on race days. A compromise was reached whereby small gates were inserted in the blocking banks and kept locked at all times except on days when race meetings were being held. Thus the curious features on a Dark Age Dyke were explained as the result of an eighteenth-century conflict between transport and recreation. Once again, while not of importance by itself, this does show how documentary evidence can interpret the earthworks that the field archaeologist discovers. It also stresses the existence of relatively modern features which can and do puzzle the archaeologist.[25]

It is perhaps worth noting that a large proportion of the earthwork remains that are found, and which need to be interpreted, are of post-medieval date. Not only does a large proportion of shrunken or shifted villages, and even deserted villages, fall into this category, but many other sites as well. Much of the ridge and furrow to be studied is, strictly, post-medieval or much of it was last ploughed after the end of the medieval period. There is also a whole series of temporary earthwork fortifications dating from the seventeenth-century Civil War period that are really part of

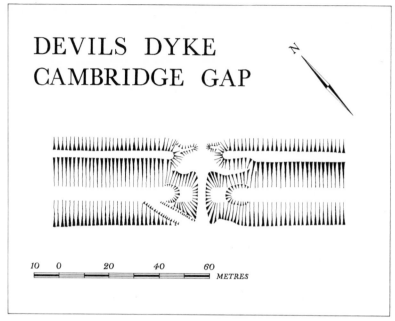

60 *Detail of the Cambridge Gap, Devil's Dyke, Cambridgeshire, showing the eighteenth-century blocking of the medieval cut.*

the field archaeologist's province, while countless minor copse banks, house sites and ponds are all of fairly recent origin. These ought to be recorded, interpreted and dated if only to avoid their being confusingly assigned to much earlier periods. They often require documentary research to explain them, though this is usually not very difficult. Thus a huge earthen dam, up to 5 m. high and 15 m. wide which spans a valley near Slipton, in Northamptonshire, can be easily dated by documents. Two maps of the late eighteenth century showing the area do this. One depicts all the fields, but shows no dam, only the name Plumwell Lawn, where it now stands. The other shows the same area, with the dam and its lake in existence. Indeed though it is not known with certainty, the maps were probably made to depict various alterations and improvements to the area which included the dam and its lake.

Another important type of earthwork remains, which only recently has been recognised as extremely common, is that of abandoned formal gardens of the sixteenth, seventeenth and early eighteenth centuries. Most of the history of English gardens and garden design has been carried out by historians using the existing gardens of great houses, together with surviving documents. A much better history of garden design could be written by field archaeologists carrying out detailed examination of the hundreds of gardens of all periods, which still exist buried in woodland or on waste ground. These were abandoned for various reasons without having the constant alterations of later times, which is a common feature of existing gardens (*61*). Once found, and they are not difficult to recognise given some knowledge of the history of gardens, documents especially maps can often help us to interpret them in detail. At Tarrant Gunville in Dorset, air photographs, fieldwork and survey enabled the Royal Commission on Historical Monuments to discover and make a plan of the remarkable early eighteenth-century gardens, designed by Charles Bridgeman, around Eastbury House. A comparison with the original designs, preserved in the Gough Manuscripts, showed how their final layout differed from these. It was also possible to appreciate the enormous engineering and earth-moving works which were involved in the actual construction of a sophisticated design of canals, basins, octagonal mounts, *parterres* and terraces on a piece of rolling chalk downland.[26]

In Northamptonshire, elaborate though partially destroyed late-sixteenth-century garden remains at Lyveden were surveyed. The results were then compared with Sir Thomas Tresham's published letters, giving

61 Site of house and gardens, Harrington, Northamptonshire
*Most of these well-preserved earthworks are the gardens of a house which stood in the
centre of the picture. They probably date from the late sixteenth or seventeenth
centuries.*

detailed orders for their construction. From this it has been possible to understand for the first time the very advanced design proposed there, and incidentally the existing buildings have been put into their true perspective. In addition the work has revealed the unfinished nature of the site which accords well with the known facts concerning Tresham's death.[27]

In Cambridgeshire there is a puzzling arrangement of terraces, dams, platforms, ditches and scarps on a piece of waste heathland at Gamlingay. These were not only explained by a map showing the original house and garden, built and laid out here around 1720 by Sir George Downing, but the plan was proved incorrect in some aspects. It was seen to be only an idealised layout, unrelated to the actual ground, which had to be altered to fit the natural features of the area when the actual construction work was started.[28] This again shows the value of combining fieldwork with documentary research by which both aspects of the study benefit greatly.

Perhaps the most important and certainly the most difficult of all medieval sites to explain are deserted or shrunken villages. Up till now we have dealt only with their discovery and recording, and the interpretation of names and minor details. But when we move on to explain their history and to find out why and when such villages declined, were abandoned or moved, we must have a basic understanding of documents, and appreciate their actual value and relevance to our problems.

Before using the documents that purport to tell us the history of any deserted medieval village we have to know why these documents were made and the basis on which the information in them was compiled. It is usually necessary to learn something of the efficiency or otherwise of the administrative or legal machinery that brought them into being. Thus the fact that a village is not mentioned by name in Domesday Book, the earliest source of information for most places, does not necessarily prove that the village did not exist in 1086. It may mean, and often does, that the details of that village are listed under the entry for another place. The clerks who compiled Domesday Book were interested in who held land and within what manor. They were not making a complete gazeteer of English villages. Likewise if Domesday Book records a village with a relatively large population and today it consists only of a farm, or two or three houses, it again does not necessarily indicate that the village has been deserted. In many parts of the country it means only that the entry in Domesday Book in that name included a host of other farms and hamlets scattered over the adjoining area, merely because of their tenurial relationship to it at that time.

This kind of problem occurs again and again in later documents, when, as a result of variations in tenure, or for purely administrative reasons, either a number of settlements are grouped together under one name or a single village is split up into parts which are described separately. The constant division of large manors into separate smaller ones as well as the reverse can often reduce manorial documents to useless pieces of parchment for the medieval archaeologist who is trying to establish size or wealth.

The records of taxation compiled by the medieval central administration, such as Subsidy Rolls and Poll Tax Returns, are more useful, but still need careful interpretation. Not only were they compiled on constantly-changing bases, but evasion and corruption were known to be widespread. There is remarkable evidence from the deserted medieval village of Upton, in Gloucestershire, that though the village was already depopulated in 1383–84 its tax quota to the central government was being paid by the Lord of the Manor. This is the kind of situation that needs to be remembered and considered by all workers in the field.[29] Any potential historian of deserted medieval villages must first read widely on the background to documents before tackling the documents themselves.

The beginner may also waste a great deal of time collecting information which has little or no value in explaining his particular site. The easiest documents to use, largely because they have been printed by local Record Societies, the Record Commissioners or the Public Record Office, are Feet of Fines, Patent and Close Rolls and Manorial accounts. From these there is rarely any detailed information about the villages as such, but it is often possible to draw up a seemingly complete descent of the manors or manor of the village. The result is that many descriptions of deserted medieval villages include interminable lists of obscure lords who often never visited the place, and who had no effect on the life of that village. In any case it is usually extremely difficult to track down all the sub-manors, whose holders may have influenced the village history, and only the tenants-in-chief, often two or three times removed in the feudal hierarchy, can be traced. Such manorial descents are of little value, and the detailed listing of such people is worth while only when it can be *proved* that a lord actually did something to the village besides collecting rents, such as evicting tenants or converting arable land to pasture.

This is not to say that the laborious work of tracing manors is never useful. It is sometimes the only way to solve some problems. Thus in Wiltshire, a deserted settlement which lies around More Farm in White-parish could not be traced back before the early thirteenth century under its name of More. However, by building up a complex manorial descent from a host of various documents it was possible to identify it under a different name in Domesday Book.[30] While manorial descents should sometimes be worked out, there is no need to inflict the whole list on a potential reader of the final report.

Clearly the most important part of the field archaeologist's work on documents relating to deserted medieval villages is to establish the relative size of each village and the date and reasons for its decline and abandonment. With certain places this is easy because they were deliberately destroyed or removed at a late date and for specific reasons, which are well documented. The best examples of these are the villages, and even small towns, which were removed as a result of emparking in the eighteenth or nineteenth centuries. The classic example of this is at Milton Abbas, in Dorset, where between 1771 and 1790 the whole town was removed and replaced by a magnificent landscaped park.[31] Less well known but in the same county is the village of More Crichel, which was swept away soon after 1765 for the same reason.[32] In Oxfordshire the village of Nuneham Courtney also disappeared in 1760–2 as a result of emparking.[33]

Another is the village of Croxton in Cambridgeshire. On the Enclosure Map of the parish for 1811, Croxton village is shown as still lying along its main street in front of the hall. By 1834 it had all gone and a new park appeared around the hall and now isolated church.[34] Yet the story is not as simple as it appears. On the ground, the remains of the houses, standing in 1811, still exist as does the main street, now a holloway. But there are also other earthworks which show that the village was once much bigger and had declined dramatically long before the nineteenth-century emparking.

This feature is a recurring one whatever the alleged date of the desertion of a village. The great majority of deserted medieval villages did not disappear suddenly as a result of pestilence or enclosure. They gradually declined often from a host of social and economic reasons and were thus very small when they were finally killed as a result of other events. Thus to say that a village was deserted as a result of enclosure by a prosperous sixteenth-century sheep farmer, because a document tells us this, is only one part of the story. Ideally we need to know the size and prosperity of the village for the previous two or three centuries, both in actual terms and in relation to its neighbours which have survived, before we can put the final enclosure and depopulation into its true context. Therefore when we use documents to explain how and when a village disappeared we must not take just one piece of evidence, however convincing it may be, and assume that it explains everything.

For example an Inquisition Post-Mortem of 1349, concerning the village of Cowesfield Louvras in Wiltshire, now deserted, tells us that at that date all the tenants were dead from the plague and only three freeholders remained there. These latter were subsequently removed and so we have apparently good evidence for the final desertion of the village. But by 1361 another Inquisition Post Mortem informs us that 'divers tenants' of the village were paying 53 shillings and fourpence in rent. Obviously the village was resettled and continued to exist. The actual date of its desertion is unknown, but as it had always been small and the plague presumably weakened it still further, it was probably abandoned gradually over a long period of time.[35]

In order to establish the reasons for, and the time of, desertion of a village, the trends of prosperity and population over centuries must be traced. In addition it is necessary to note the occurrence of specific events which may have caused the final abandonment. This is much easier said than done, for with any particular deserted village the documents that tell us these facts were either not written or have not survived, quite apart from the difficulties in the interpretation of those that have. The field archaeologist will be very fortunate if he ever obtains a complete picture of the history of a deserted village from documents. It is only by taking large areas covering numerous existing as well as deserted villages, that general trends can be established. The admirable work on these lines of the Deserted Medieval Village Research Group, covering whole counties, shows this well, for in most cases even they are defeated by individual sites.[36]

No one village ever has a complete run of records detailing its history and some none at all. There are three small deserted settlements of Mill, Mallows and West Cotton in Raunds, Northamptonshire. The only record of their existence comes from manorial accounts, Inquisitions Post-Mortem, Close Rolls and Estate Maps, but none of these documents gives any indication of the size, prosperity or period of abandonment of these villages. Even so this type of document ought to be looked at and while not always of great value may produce a useful piece of information.

Thus the deserted village of Lazerton, near Stourpaine, Dorset, has a recorded population of 7, i.e. perhaps a total population of 20 to 30, in Domesday Book. From then until 1428, when it was not taxed because it had less than 10 inhabitants, we know nothing of its size or prosperity. After that only the Hearth Tax Returns of 1662 tell us that it was abandoned except for the still existing farm. But from a twelfth-century charter we know that the church there was so poor at that time that it was released from paying its ecclesiastical dues. This piece of information shows that the village was not removed suddenly, perhaps in the fourteenth century, but was a tiny settlement which gradually declined over the centuries for reasons which are as yet not entirely clear.[37]

This point cannot be stressed too often. Villages were finally abandoned for a whole host of separate reasons. Some were cleared away by Cistercian sheep farmers in the twelfth and thirteenth centuries.[38] Some were burnt and ravaged in the course of wars, especially in the north of England by Scots invaders.[39] Plagues and certainly the Black Death of 1349 and after sometimes took their toll.[40] Many villages received a death blow from the development of sheep farming in the fifteenth and sixteenth centuries.[41] Emparking of land round great houses from the sixteenth to the nineteenth centuries resulted in the removal of others. Even more recently the village of Snap, in Wiltshire, lost the last of its inhabitants in 1913. Yet the vast majority of these villages were small, poor and already in decline long before the events took place which led to their final abandonment. The clearance of villages by the Army during the last World War, such as Imber on Salisbury Plain, Tyneham in South Dorset, and Stanford, West Tofts and Tottington in Norfolk, was achieved at a time of national emergency only because they were relatively small. Earthworks at all of these villages show that shrinkage had been taking place long before the Army took over their sites.

Though the deserted medieval villages have taken priority in the work of the medieval field archaeologists and others, in fact the most common earthworks will be those associated with a flourishing village. These places are usually and often misleadingly termed shrunken villages. They can vary from a single open space covered by platforms, banks and scarps lying between existing houses in the village street, to large areas of earthworks lying around or to one side of a village. Yet these remains are the most difficult of all to interpret and understand and on the whole documents usually fail to enlighten us. We are mainly thrown back to topographical interpretation with all its lack of precision.

Sometimes, if the abandonment of houses has taken place relatively recently, estate maps and even early Ordnance Survey maps can date it. Thus the earthworks in the village of Woolland, in Dorset, are shown as houses on the first edition Ordnance Survey one inch map of 1811.[42] The 1800 Enclosure Map of the village of Luddington in the Brook, Northamptonshire, shows houses lying along both sides of a small stream. Today only the church and one farm are there and the rest of the community has moved to a drier site on the hillside above. Usually however when the abandonment of part of the village has taken place at an early date, there is no way of finding out from documents when or why it happened. Sometimes the documents can give some clue that shows that the village had been generally declining in size and prosperity for centuries, but more often the problem lies in the fact that the remains we find today are not the result of shrinkage at all, but merely movement.

In fact the more one examines the earthworks of former habitation around existing villages, the more one appreciates that settlements are living entities which can and do move about, contract and expand as well as merely die. In some cases a village can actually slide sideways and take up a completely new position, though the reasons why it does this may be hard to find. One such is Caxton, in Cambridge, which is now a long street village on either side of the Old North Road (*62*). The parish church stands remote from the village but surrounded by a set of old lanes and holloways, earthworks and scatters of medieval pottery in the arable land. Here the village has undoubtedly moved from its original site to the main road when the latter became an important routeway. The movement perhaps took place around 1247 when a charter granting a weekly market to the Lord of the Manor was obtained, but we cannot be certain. Indeed the market may only reflect the completion of the move which had been slowly taking place over previous centuries.

Again the ground tells us more than the documents about this move, for the closes and gardens behind the existing houses are long curved strips, which not only look like former holdings in the medieval fields, but meet the adjacent ridge and furrow end on. It seems that when the village moved it was actually laid out on the existing strips of its own fields.[43] However such deductions are moving beyond the realms of field archaeology towards total archaeology—a different, if related, discipline (see pp. 150–1).

On rare occasions documents can be of use when fieldwork fails. At Landbeach, in Cambridgeshire, the present village is almost divided in two by fields containing a series of abandoned house platforms. Here by good fortune the whole history has survived in a series of remarkably complete documents. This part of the village was removed in the mid-sixteenth century by one Richard Kirby when he was enclosing land for sheep. The resulting furore, which took place as the village was a large one, led to the exact details being written down. These in turn survive because the other major landowner in the parish was Corpus Christi College, Cambridge, a perpetual institution whose archives have remained intact.[44]

So far we have been concerned with the interpretation of deserted, shrunken and moved villages in terms of when and why the desertion, shrinkage or movement took place. Yet even after a site has ceased to provide a living place for people, it is not entirely abandoned. Events still take place there which leave traces on the ground and which need to be interpreted. At the simplest level, ponds are dug, new fields are laid out across it and later trackways run over it. All these may be established by ground examination alone, though maps and other later documents can assist.

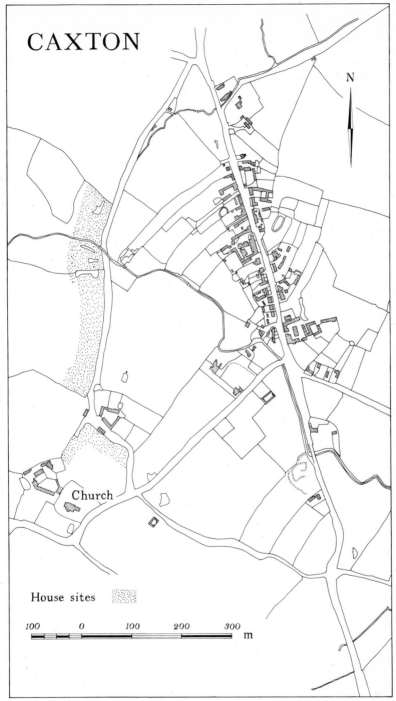

CAXTON

N

Church

House sites

100   0   100   200   300
m

62 *Caxton village, Cambridgeshire.*

The classic case of this is the deserted village of Papley in Northampton-shire (*50*). Historians and field archaeologists have combined to establish the whole development and decline of this place as a village. It lies on high boulder clay-land in a remote corner of the parish of Warmington, nearly three miles from Warmington village. Its name, *Pappas Leah* or the clearing of Pappa, suggests that it grew up as a daughter hamlet of Warmington, as the land of the parish was gradually reclaimed from the woodlands and waste. Though its name is not recorded in documents of the twelfth century, it is possible to identify it in Domesday Book as a small place, listed under Warmington, and having a recorded population of three villeins. That is, it was then only a hamlet of three farmsteads. In 1301 we know there were 12 taxpayers in the village, but it was clearly still very small. In 1456 the village and manor were sold to William Brown, a wealthy wool merchant from Stamford in Lincolnshire, and he left it to his daughter in 1495. She and her husband destroyed seven houses in the village and enclosed 200 acres of its fields. In 1539 their son was charged with enclosing more land and in court witnesses testified that there had once been ten houses and four cottages in the village, though only two houses remained. Today two isolated and widely separated farms both of nineteenth-century date exist in the area.

On the ground the site of the village can easily be identified, lying half way between the two modern farms. Even on a map, its position is pin-pointed by a host of footpaths which meet near the stream. Here we can find the large U-shaped ditch, called 'moat' on Ordnance Survey maps, a holloway or street and various platforms, banks and scarps indicative of a deserted medieval village. There are also two derelict eighteenth-century cottages. Yet the history of Papley did not end in the sixteenth century as soon becomes clear when we look at later documents. The first of these is a fine map of 1632 which shows a large and palatial manor house and its gardens near a moat, surrounded by farm buildings. There is also a cottage shown on the site of the present cottages. On a map of 1685 this manor house is shown as ruinous, though the farm buildings and the cottages are still there. The County Historian, writing in 1720, said there were three cottages there at that time. By 1802 further changes had taken place as another map shows. A new farmstead had been built on the old site, other farm buildings erected and the eighteenth-century cottages were in existence. This situation remained until the middle of the nineteenth century when, as local tradition tells us, the farmhouse was burnt down and the present farms were built on new sites. The two cottages remained inhabited until a few years ago.

If with this later evidence we look at the remaining earthworks again, we now see a different picture. The 'moat' is part of the seventeenth-century manor house garden. The holloway is the approach track to the last farm on the site, and all but one of the splendid building platforms can be identified as eighteenth-century farm buildings. In fact very little of the surface remains were part of the village and future excavators will no doubt find considerable difficulty in recovering its fragments from under the later alterations and disturbances. This kind of example should make all medieval field archaeologists careful of being overdogmatic about any site.

Detailed work of this type may seem to be beyond the average field archaeologist, but it is not. A remarkable piece of work, carried out on these lines, though sadly little known due to its rather obscure publication, is that carried out on the remains of the shrunken village of Strixton, in North-amptonshire.[45]

Here within an area of just under seven hectares, every single disturbance of the ground was recorded, mapped and interpreted. These included not only the more obvious and important remains of medieval houses and gardens, roads, manor house site, seventeenth-century gardens and ridge and furrow but eighteenth-century ponds, nineteenth-century quarries, sixteenth-century meadow ditches, late-nineteenth-century limestone pits and a Victorian well. Even a 1930s tennis court and two Second World War Nissen hut platforms were noted and interpreted. The final result is not only a monumental example of good field archaeology, but a valuable piece of historical research in explaining the total archaeology of a group of apparently undistinguished small pasture fields.

So far, this chapter has been rightly concerned with the interpretation and explanation of sites using documents in their usually accepted sense, that is those written down on parchment or paper. However there are other documents of a different type which sometimes can and should be used. These are more permanent documents such as gravestones, memorials and heraldic devices, usually carved in stone or worked in plaster, which, by their relationship to an archaeological site, or their literary content, can help in the interpretation of that site. There are a number of ways in which this type of 'document' can be used. A very simple instance, noted by the writer on a number of occasions, is that where churchyards have been extended over adjacent house platforms and holloways within shrunken or moved villages. Here the age of the earliest gravestones gives a date by when we can be sure the earthworks were abandoned.

A more complex example of the use of this kind of documentation is to be seen at the moat and associated earthworks around the Manor House at Papworth St Agnes, in Cambridgeshire.[46] The moat is certainly medieval in origin, but careful fieldwork on some inconsistencies revealed that it was later turned into a garden. At some time in the post-medieval period it had 'prospect mounds' erected within the angles of the moat, a long 'canal' or pond inserted within it and outer embanked enclosures added to one side. These features must obviously relate to the house still standing within the moat, which can be dated architecturally to the late sixteenth century. However the fine plaster ceilings in the house have cartouches containing the arms of the Mallory family, as well as the letters W.M. These not only allow us to suggest that the house, and therefore its garden, were built between 1585 and 1614, when two successive William Mallories were alive, but it also gives us a starting point to investigate the history and social status of this family. In this way we can begin to understand the kind of people who constructed the house and garden, and so explain the mere earthworks in terms of social history.

7 Publication of fieldwork

In this book we have been concerned with the importance of finding, recording and interpreting medieval sites. Inevitably this is the most complex and certainly the most rewarding part of medieval field archaeology. By following the somewhat sketchy methods outlined in the previous chapters and with experience gained from constant practice the medieval field archaeologist will soon build up a large collection of information contained in maps, photographs, plans, cards and files.

All this is splendid, but it is only half the battle. However good the fieldwork and documentary research, it is of no value if the results are then carefully hidden away in the archaeologist's filing cabinet. The results of all fieldwork and indeed excavation or any form of archaeological research must be passed on in one form or another, so that other workers both now and in the future can make use of it.

This may seem an obvious and unnecessary point to make. It ought to be, but unfortunately it is not. There is a common and regrettable tendency amongst many local archaeologists carefully to hoard the results of their work so that little of it ever sees the light of day. Sometimes this is due to the inevitable pressures of other activities which prevent the worker from sorting out and writing up his results. It may be the lack of outlets for the work, though more often it is the inability, actual or assumed, to commit ideas to paper. Frequently it is an unwillingness to let others 'poach' the results of years of hard work. Whatever the reasons, there can be no excuse for not passing on the information gained during fieldwork to other archaeologists. It can and must be done if our chosen subject is to advance. All work, of whatever standard, must be written up and made available in some form to other workers.

Naturally the first thought for most people is that they must publish their work as fully as possible. This is a very laudable aim, but they will probably quickly find that it is easier said than done. The obvious place to publish medieval archaeological fieldwork is in the local county journal. However there are problems. Some counties do not have a local society which publishes a journal regularly. Others that do unfortunately still need persuading that the results of this type of work are just as important as those of the inevitable excavation on a Roman site, or as the thousands of worked flints discovered on ploughed fields.

Even more formidable is the task of publishing in the present inflationary situation. As anyone who is involved in the production of archaeological journals knows the cost of publishing even a slim work by normal methods is rapidly increasing. One page of printed text in an average sized book can cost as much as £10. At these prices, anything that is published must not only be well worth printing, but must be written as concisely as possible. The result is that even when sites, which seem to be important, can be published, they will probably have to be given no more than two or three lines of text. This in one sense is no bad thing for it forces the writer to compress his results into a length that it probably really deserves if a broad overall view is taken. In any case the archaeological world at large suffers from literary verbosity, and inflation may be one unexpected way of controlling this.

The medieval field archaeologist is then unlikely to be able to publish his results in any great detail in the normal archaeological journals. However many organisations do produce less lavish publications either by offset litho or cyclostyle printing, which have a wide circulation. These vary greatly in size, content and especially the area they cover, but any potential fieldworker may check if such publications cover his area. Some local archaeological groups produce newsletters which include lists of all work done in their areas. For example Buckinghamshire is covered by the *Milton Keynes Journal* (formerly the Wolverton and District Arch. Soc.); Northamptonshire by the *Bulletin of the Northamptonshire Federation of Archaeological Societies*; and all south-west England by the *Archaeological Review*, published by the C.B.A. Groups 12 and 13. The editors of all these and similar works are only too pleased to receive short notes about fieldwork. Once again the amount of detail that can be put into such journals and newsletters is restricted and most will only accept a few lines. Therefore much information still cannot be published in full.

The answer to this problem is to place the results of fieldwork in easily accessible archives where they can be consulted by other people. There are various places where such archives exist and where the information will be welcome in one form or another. Most local museums keep records of discoveries, sometimes only on large-scale maps, but in many cases they are prepared to accept written accounts, photographs and other material. Even if this material is published or sent elsewhere, it is advisable to let the museum have as much detail as they can take, for the more places in which the information is available the better.

A more important archive, in that it has a national basis and wide access, is the Archaeological Division of the Ordnance Survey. The Record Cards and Maps that the Division holds in its offices at Southampton, together with copies of the Record Cards in the National Monuments Record in London, constitute the major national archaeological archives. As was pointed out in the first chapter, this is a basic source of information for the field archaeologist of all periods which must be consulted before work starts. When the fieldwork is completed there is no better way to repay the debt than by passing the new information back to the archives so that they can be kept up to date. The Ordnance Survey is always willing to accept the results of fieldwork and incorporate them in their records. Once more however the fieldworker ought to remember that the information he sends has to be reduced to a standard format to fit the record cards, and he would be well advised to summarise his results concisely rather than expect the Ordnance Survey to wade through masses of undigested information.

Potentially a most useful archive in which to place results of all archaeological work is the recently formed Archaeological Record Section of the National Monuments Record. Here all information, however detailed, including plans and photographs, but not finds, will be accepted and made accessible to all. Even so this should not be regarded as an excuse for unloading all one's notes made over a long period of time. Some of the records already received there are of this nature and though potentially of great value are extremely difficult to understand and use by other people. Wherever the field archaeological results go and whatever they may consist of they must be sorted out, written up and if possible neatly typed with the relevant photographs or plans clearly labelled and cross referenced to the text. It cannot be stressed too much that the fieldworker has a duty to present the results of his efforts in a clearly understandable and readable form so that the process of studying the remains of the medieval past can be continued.

The same applies to any finds made during fieldwork. Ideally they should be given to the local museum, but understandably many people like to keep at least the more interesting finds themselves. This is not necessarily a bad thing, though it helps all concerned in the future if the material is described, drawn and photographed where necessary and these records deposited with the other written accounts. If the collection is large and of some importance, formal arrangements should be made for its ultimate deposition in a museum, to avoid it being broken up and dispersed. Finally, and most important, all finds must be marked, labelled and boxed so that ultimately they can be easily identified and stored.

8 Towards total archaeology

The methods of work for the medieval field archaeologist, outlined in the foregoing chapters, may well be quite enough for the beginner. He may feel that by detailed fieldwork, field survey and documentary research, which leads to the discovery and interpretation of many new sites, he has both fulfilled himself personally and played his part in the recovery of knowledge of the medieval past.

Yet he ought, as he goes about his chosen task, to become aware that he is involved not only in the understanding of individual sites where man has worked and lived, but is also becoming involved in the understanding of the relationships between sites. A good survey of a deserted medieval village should include the surrounding ridge and furrow, which represents its fields. The plan and description of a deer park must contain details of obviously later banks and ditches connected with woodland management. Yet ultimately there is even more to field archaeology than this. There is the final deciphering of the total landscape.

The recognition of field shapes to find deserted settlements, or medieval deer parks, should make the archaeologist aware that fields everywhere have shapes and forms directly related to the history of the landscape of which they form part. Likewise a survey of ridge and furrow and strip lynchets, when correlated with old estate maps, should enable him to realise it is possible by delving deeper into these matters to ultimately trace the ebb and flow of agriculture in an area for 2,000 years. By trying to explain the remains of the abandoned house sites on one side of an existing village he is becoming aware of the complex history of medieval villages which could and did move about often over considerable distances.

In fact it should dawn on the field archaeologist that he, better than most people, has the experience and ability to draw together the threads of individual archaeological sites, which, when woven with the evidence of field shapes, place names, architecture, geology and village forms, make up the complete landscape we see today. By looking carefully at railway stations and churches as well as deserted villages, by noting eighteenth-century field shapes as well as thirteenth-century strip lynchets and by studying nineteenth-century census returns as well as Domesday Book it is possible to build up a picture of how the total landscape or the total archaeology of the landscape has evolved throughout the historic period and even the prehistoric and Roman periods too.[1]

Such study of course involves much more than the mere principles of field archaeology which are our concern in this book. It means working on a whole host of disciplines such as social and economic history, geomorphology, geology, art history, industrial archaeology and many more. It is by no means an easy path to follow, but the rewards are immense even in the most unpromising areas. The Fenlands of eastern England for example are by no means everyone's idea of rural England. Their monotonous flat appearance and their alleged recent history, apparently dating from the seventeenth-century drainage schemes, repels both the casual visitor and the interested archaeologist. But if the methods of Total Archaeology are brought to bear on such a landscape it can be almost completely deciphered. Today after studying a small area of typical Cambridgeshire Fenland, everything of its past is clear to me as I stand and look at it. I can point to areas of prehistoric settlement, identify prehistoric rivers, Roman canals and medieval fields. I can see seventeenth-century, eighteenth-century and nineteenth-century fields, date all the main drainage ditches from the Roman period to 1940 and find the sites of windpumps (43) and the foundations of nineteenth-century steam engines. All this and much more is still waiting in the modern landscape for the Total Field Archaeologist wherever he lives.

Abbreviations used in References and Bibliography

Ag. Hist. Rev.   Agricultural History Review
Arch. Cantiana   Archaeologia Cantiana
Arch. J.   Archaeological Journal
Arch. Newsletter   Archaeological Newsletter
Ass. Arch. Soc. Reps. and Paps.   Associated Architectural Societies Reports and Papers
Brit. Mus. Quarterly   British Museum Quarterly
Cornish Arch.   Cornish Archaeology
Derby Arch. J.   Derbyshire Archaeological Journal
Econ. Hist. Rev.   Economic History Review
Geog. J.   Geographical Journal
Med. Arch.   Medieval Archaeology
Norfolk Arch.   Norfolk Archaeology
Northants. Nat. Hist. Soc.   Northamptonshire Natural History Society
O.S.   Ordnance Survey
Post Med. Arch.   Post Medieval Archaeology
Procs. Cambs. Ant. Soc.   Proceedings of the Cambridge Antiquarian Society
Procs. Dorset Arch. Soc.   Proceedings of the Dorset Natural History and Archaeological Society
Procs. Hants. F.C.   Proceedings of the Hampshire Field Club
Procs. Suffolk Inst. Arch.   Proceedings of the Suffolk Institute of Archaeology
Procs. Univ. Bristol Spel. Soc.   Proceedings of the University of Bristol Speleological Society
P.S.A.S.   Proceedings of the Society of Antiquaries of Scotland
Reps. and Paps. Lincs. Archit. and Arch. Soc.   Reports and Papers of the Lincolnshire Architectural and Archaeological Society
R.C.H.M.   Royal Commission on Historical Monuments (England)
R.C.A.M. (Scot.)   Royal Commission on Ancient Monuments (Scotland)
R.C.A.M. (Wales)   Royal Commission on Ancient Monuments (Wales)
Surrey Arch. Coll.   Surrey Archaeological Collections

Sussex Arch. Coll.   Sussex Archaeological Collections

Trans. Birmingham Arch. Soc.   Transactions of the Birmingham Archaeological Society

Trans. Bristol and Gloucs. Arch. Soc.   Transactions of the Bristol and
Gloucestershire Archaeological Society

Trans. Leics. Arch. and Hist. Soc.   Transactions of the Leicestershire
Archaeological and Historical Society

Trans. London and Middlesex Arch. Soc.   Transactions of the London and
Middlesex Archaeological Society

Trans. Newbury and District F.C.   Transactions of the Newbury and District Field Club

Trans. Radnorshire Soc.   Transactions of the Radnorshire Society

Trans. Woolhope Natur. F.C.   Transactions of the Woolhope Naturalists
Field Club

V.C.H.   Victoria County History

W.A.M.   Wiltshire Archaeological Magazine

References

Introduction

1 Atkinson, R. J. C. *Field Archaeology* (1953).
2 Coles, J. *Field Archaeology in Britain* (1972).
3 Ashbee, P. 'Field Archaeology: Its Origins and Development', in Fowler, P. J. (Ed.), *Archaeology and the Landscape* (1972), 38–74.

Chapter 1

1 *Antiquity*, 45 (1971), 298–9.
2 Crawford, O. G. S. *Air Photography for Archaeologists* (1929); St Joseph, J. K. S. (Ed.) *The Uses of Air Photography* (1966).
1 R.C.H.M., *Dorset* II (1970), Corfe Castle (10), p. 78.

Chapter 3

1 Crawford, O. G. S. and Keiller, A. *Wessex from the Air* (1928).
2 Bowen, H. C. *Ancient Fields* (1961), 64, appendix c has a tally card for strip fields; Beresford, M. W. and Hurst, J. G. *Deserted Medieval Villages* (1972), 315–17 has a tabular list for deserted villages.
3 Cookson, M. B. *Photography for Archaeologists* (1954).
4 Hammond, N. 'A giant scale for long-distance photography', *Antiquity*, 47 (1973), 144.
5 R.C.H.M., *West Cambridgeshire* (1968), Knapwell (11), Plate 2.
6 Tebbut, C. F. 'Two Newly Discovered Medieval Sites', *Sussex Arch. Coll.* 110 (1972), 31–6.
7 Grinsell. L. V. *The Ancient Burial Mounds of England* (1953), 102.
8 Atkinson, R. J. C. *Field Archaeology* (1953), University of Durham; *Surveying for Archaeologists* (1960).
9 Dilke, D. A. W. *The Roman Land Surveyors* (1971), 16, 49 and 50.
10 R.C.H.M., *Dorset* III (1970), Sturminster Newton (69).
11 R.C.H.M., *Newark on Trent* (1964), Figs. 11 and 12.
12 Atkinson, R. J. C. *Field Archaeology* (1953).

Chapter 4—

1 Beresford, M. W. and St Joseph, J. K. S., *Medieval England: An Aerial Survey* (1958), 234–5.

2 Barker, P. and Lawson, J., 'A Pre-Norman Field-System at Hen Domen', *Med. Arch.*, 15 (1971), 58–72.

3 Taylor, C. C. 'Cambridgeshire Earthwork Surveys', *Procs. Cambs. Ant. Soc.*, 64 (1973), 37–8.

4 Bonney, D. J. 'Former Farms and Fields at Challacombe', in Gregory, K. J. and Ravenhill, W. (Eds.) *Exeter Essays in Geography* (1971), 83–91.

5 R.C.H.M., *Dorset* III (1970), Turnworth (6).

6 R.C.H.M., op cit, Ibberton (10).

7 R.C.H.M., *West Cambridgeshire* (1968), Childerley (2) and (4).

8 R.C.H.M., *Dorset* III (1970), Puddletown (21).

9 Beresford, M. W. and Hurst, J. G. *Deserted medieval villages* (1971), 117–31.

10 R.C.H.M., *Huntingdonshire* (1926), Huntingdon (6).

11 R.C.H.M., *Dorset* II (1970), Dorchester (228).

12 R.C.H.M., *Newark on Trent, The Civil War Siegeworks* (1964), 34 (4).

13 Taylor, C. C. 'Cambridgeshire Earthwork Surveys', *Procs. Cambs. Ant Soc.*, 64 (1973), 38–41.

14 R.C.H.M., *Dorset* III (1970), Manston (9).

15 R.C.H.M., *West Cambridgeshire* (1968), Orwell (24) and (41).

16 R.C.H.M., *North East Cambridgeshire* (1972), Reach (23) and (37).

17 R.C.H.M., *Dorset* III (1970), Milton Abbas (24).

18 Hooper, M. D. *et al*, *Hedges and Local History* (1971).

19 Bowen, H. C. and Taylor, C. C. 'The Site of Newton, Studland, Dorset', *Med. Arch.*, 8 (1964), 223–6.

20 Taylor, C. C. 'Strip Lynchets', *Antiquity*, XL (1966), 280.

21 Crawford, O. G. S. and Keiller, A. *Wessex from the Air* (1928), 68–71.

22 R.C.H.M., *Monuments Threatened and Destroyed* (1963), 2.

23 R.C.H.M., *Dorset* III (1970), Winterborne Houghton (7) and (9).

24 Brown, A. E. 'The Castle, Borough and Port of Cenllys, *Trans. Radnor Soc.*, 42 (1972), 11–22.

25 R.C.H.M., *Dorset* II (1970), Celtic Field Groups 1, 14 and 23; Fowler, P. J. and Bowen, H. C. 'The Archaeology of Fyfield and Overton Downs, Wilts., *W.A.M.*, 58 (1963), 104–6; Crawford, O. G. S. and Keiller, A. *Wessex from the Air* (1928), 124–5, 140–1.

26 R.C.H.M., *North East Cambridgeshire* (1972), Horningsea (29) and (33).

27 R.C.H.M., *West Cambridgeshire* (1968), Bourn (43), Plate 2.

28 R.C.H.M., *Dorset* III (1970), Sturminster Newton (47).

29 Bowen, H. C. and Fowler, P. J. 'Roman Settlements in Wessex' in *Rural Settlement in Roman Britain* (1960).

30 R.C.H.M., *Shielings and Bastles* (1970), 12–14.

31 Knipe's Map of Stamford, Lincolnshire, 1833.

32 *Bulletin of the Northamptonshire Federation of Archaeological Societies*, 7 (1972), 4.

33 Wadmore, B. *The Earthworks of Bedfordshire* (1920), 145–9.

34 R.C.H.M., *West Cambridgeshire* (1968), xlxvi.

35 Fox, C. *Offa's Dyke* (1955); Fox, C. and Fox, A. 'Wansdyke Reconsidered', *Arch. J.*, 115 (1958), 1–48.

36 Fox, C. *The Archaeology of the Cambridge Region* (1923), 124–5; R.C.H.M., *North East Cambridgeshire* (1972), appendix 1.

37 R.C.H.M., *West Cambridgeshire* (1968), lxiii.

38 R.C.H.M., op cit, Caxton (19).

39   Fowler, P. J. 'A Rectangular Earthwork Enclosure at Wick Farm, Tisbury, Wilts.', *Antiquity*, 37 (1963), 290–3.
40   Bowen, H. C. and Fowler, P. J. 'Roman Settlements in Wessex', in *Rural Settlement in Roman Britain* (1960).
41   R.C.H.M., *West Cambridgeshire* (1968), Knapwell (11) and Wimpole (20).
42   Taylor, C. C. 'Late Roman Pastoral Farming in Wessex', *Antiquity*, 41 (1967), 304–6.
43   R.C.H.M., *Herefordshire* I (1931), St Weonards (1); Wright, T. 'Treagro and the Large Tumulus at St Weonards', *Arch. Camb.*, 3rd ser., I (1855), 168–74.
44   R.C.H.M., *West Cambridgeshire* (1968), Croydon (15) and Alexander, J. A. 'Clopton' in Mumby, L. M. (Ed.) *East Anglian Studies* (1968), 48–70.
45   Crompton, G. and Taylor, C. C. 'Earthwork Enclosures on Lakenheath Warren, West Suffolk', *Procs. Suffolk Inst. Arch.*, 32, Pt. 2 (1971), 113–20.
46   Williams, R. B. G. 'Frost and the Works of Man', *Antiquity*, 47 (1973), 19–30.
47   R.C.H.M., *Herefordshire* III (1934), Buckton (4); cf. Cross, P. 'Aspects of Glacial Geomorphology of the Wigmore and Presteigne Districts', *Trans. Woolhope Natur. Fld. Club*, 39 (1968), 202 and map 2.

Chapter 5

1   R.C.H.M., *West Cambridgeshire* (1968), lxi–lxvi.
2   R.C.H.M., *North East Cambridgeshire* (1972), Figs. 77 and 119.
3   R.C.H.M., *Dorset* III (1970), Dewlish (8).
4   Taylor, C. C. *The Cambridgeshire Landscape* (1973), 226–8;

5   Hurst, J. G. 'Deserted Medieval Villages and Excavations at Wharram Percy' in Bruce-Mitford, R. L. G. *Recent Archaeological Excavations in Britain* (1956), 251–73.
6   R.C.H.M., *A Matter of Time* (1960), Fig. 6.
7   R.C.H.M., *West Cambridgeshire* (1968), Croydon (20).
8   Allison, K. J. *et al*, *The Deserted Villages of Northamptonshire* (1966), 41.
9   Taylor, C. C. *Dorset* (1970), 49–79; Bonney, D. J. 'Pagan Saxon Burials and Boundaries in Wiltshire', *W.A.M.*, 61 (1966), 25–30; Bonney, D. J. 'Early Boundaries in Wessex' in Fowler, P. J. *Archaeology and the Landscape* (1972), 168–86.
10   Beresford, M. W. and Hurst, J. G. *Deserted Medieval Villages* (1971), 50.
11   R.C.H.M., *West Cambridgeshire* (1968), Gamlingay (62).
12   Taylor, C. C. *The Cambridgeshire Landscape* (1973), 77–90.
13   Taylor, C. C. 'Maps, Documents and Fieldwork' in Fowler, E. (Ed.) *Field Survey in British Archaeology* (1972), 56–9.
14   R.C.H.M., *Dorset* III (1971), xliv; Taylot, C. C. *Dorset* (1970), 56–9.
15   Hoskins, W. G. 'Seven Deserted Medieval Village Sites in Leicestershire', *Trans. Leics. Arch. and Hist. Soc.*, 32 (1956), 36–51.
16   Harley, J. P. 'The Evaluation of Early Maps', *Imago Mundi*, 22 (1968).
17   Beresford, M. W. and Hurst, J. G. *Deserted Medieval Villages* (1971), 50–1; Harvey, P. D. H. and Thorpe, H. *The Printed Maps of Warwickshire 1576–1900* (1959).
18   Beresford, M. W. *Med. Arch.* 10 (1966), 164–7; 11 (1967), 257–66.

19 Beresford, M. W. *History on the Ground* (1957), 198–203; R.C.H.M., *Dorset* III (1971), Milton Abbas (20).

20 R.C.H.M., *Dorset* IV (1972), Sutton Waldron (6).

21 Field, J. *English Field Names* (1972).

22 Beresford, M. W. and Hurst, J. G. *Deserted Medieval Villages* (1971), 42–3.

23 CBA, Group 4 *Annual Newsletter* (1971), 9–10.

24 R.C.H.M., *Dorset* III (1970), Dewlish (7).

25 R.C.H.M., *North East Cambridgeshire* (1972), Swaffham Bulbeck (80).

26 Fowler, P. J. 'Field Archaeology on the M5 Motorway 1969–71' in Fowler, E. (Ed.) *Field Survey in British Archaeology* (1972), 28–37.

27 Taylor, C. C. 'The Later History of the Roman Site at Hinton St Mary, Dorset', *Brit. Mus. Quarterly*, 32 (1967), 31–5.

28 *W.A.M.*, 65 (1970), 206.

29 Reaney, P. H. *Place Names of Cambridgeshire* (1942), 364, Borough Green.

30 Quoted in Beresford, M. W. and Hurst, J. G. *Deserted Medieval Villages* (1971), 50.

31 Le Patourel, H. E. J. 'Documentary Evidence and the Medieval Pottery Industry', *Med. Arch.* 12 (1968), 101–26.

32 Grundy, G. B. 'Saxon Charters of Dorset', *Procs. Dorset Arch. Soc.*, 58 (1937), 103–11; 59 (1938), 95–9, 101–7.

33 Grundy, G. B. 'Dorset Charters', *Procs. Dorset Arch. Soc.*, 55 (1933), 254–6.

34 Galbraith, V. H. *The Making of Domesday Book* (1961).

35 Hoskins, W. G. 'The Highland Zone in Domesday Book' in *Provincial England* (1965), 15–52.

36 Taylor, C. C. 'Whiteparish', *W.A.M.*, 63 (1967), 79–102.

37 Taylor, C. C. 'Lost Dorset Place Names', *Procs. Dorset Arch. Soc.*, 88 (1967), 207.

38 R.C.H.M., *Dorset* III (1971), Sturminster Newton (69).

39 Taylor, C. C. 'Lost Dorset Place Names', *Procs. Dorset Arch. Soc.*, 88 (1967), 210.

40 Ordnance Survey Record Cards, Rutland, SP 89 NE 11.

41 Biddle, M. 'Archaeology and the History of British Towns', *Antiquity*, 42 (1968), 109–116.

42 Celoria, F. and Spencer, B. W. 'Eighteenth Century Fieldwork in London and Middlesex', *Trans. London and Middlesex Arch. Soc.*, 22 (1966–70), 23–31.

Chapter 6

1 Taylor, C. C. 'Maps, Documents and Fieldwork' in Fowler, E. (Ed.) *Field Survey in British Archaeology* (1972), 50.

2 R.C.H.M., *West Cambridgeshire* (1968), Longstowe (13).

3 Beresford, M. W. *History on the Ground* (1957), 167–8.

4 Sergeantson, R. M. 'The Court Rolls of Higham Ferrers', *Ass. Arch. Soc. Reps. and Paps.*, 33 (1915–16), 95–146, 326–72; 34 (1917), 47–102.

5 R.C.H.M., *Dorset* III (1970), Piddlehinton (12); Taylor, C. C. 'Lost Dorset Place Names', *Procs. Dorset Arch. Soc.*, 88 (1966), 211–13.

6 Baker, A. R. H. and Butlin, R. A. (Eds.) *Studies of Field Systems in the British Isles* (1973).

7 R.C.H.M., *West Cambridgeshire* (1968), Lolworth (7).

158   *References*

8   R.C.H.M., *Dorset* III (1970), Turnworth (6).

9   *Ag. Hist. Rev.*, 3 (1945), 26–40; 4 (1956), 22–35.

10   R.C.H.M., *Dorset* II (1970), Corfe Castle (179).

11   R.C.H.M., *West Cambridgeshire* (1968), Wimpole (22) and p. lxvii.

12   The map and air photographs are reproduced in Baker, A. R. H. 'Co-operative Farming in Medieval England', *The Geographical Magazine*, 42 No. 7, April 1970, 500–1, and in Beresford, M. W. and St Joseph, J. K. *Medieval England: An Aerial Survey* (1958), 30–1.

13   *List of Rentals and Surveys*, P.R.O., Lists and Indexes, XXV (1908).

14   *List of Foreign Accounts*, P.R.O., Lists and Indexes, XI (1900); *List of Exchequer Accounts*, P.R.O., Lists and Indexes, XXXV (1912) etc.

15   *Calendars of Inquisitions Post Mortem*, Henry III to Edward III, 14 volumes (1904–1954); Henry VII, 4 volumes (1898–1957).

16   Unpublished in P.R.O., reference number C 143; *see* List of *Inquisitions Ad Quod Damnum*, 2 volumes, Lists and Indexes, XVII and XXII (1904–6).

17   Beresford, M. W. 'Medieval Inquisitions and the Archaeologist', *Med. Arch.*, 2 (1958), 171–3.

18   *Cal. Inq. Misc.*, II, 1307–1349, No. 143.

19   V.C.H. *Northants* III (1930), 279–80.

21   Beresford, M. W. and St Joseph, J. K. *Medieval England: An Aerial Survey* (1957), 66.

22   Lethbridge, T. 'Excavations at Burwell Castle', *Procs. Cambs. Art Soc.*, 36 (1936), 121–33; R.C.H.M., *North East Cambridgeshire* (1972), Burwell (133).

23   Fowler, P. J. 'Some Earthwork Enclosures in Wiltshire' *W.A.M.*, 60 (1965), 69–70.

24   Taylor, C. C. 'Late-Roman Pastoral Farming in Wessex', *Antiquity* 41 (1967), 304–6.

25   R.C.H.M., *North East Cambridgeshire* (1972) Appendix, p. 143.

26   R.C.H.M., *Dorset* IV (1972), Tarrant Gunville (2).

27   Brown, A. E. and Taylor, C. C. 'The Gardens at Lyveden, Northamptonshire', *Arch. J.*, 129 (1972), 154–60.

28   R.C.H.M., *West Cambridgeshire* (1968), Gamlingay (61).

29   Hilton, R. H. and Rahtz, P. A. 'Upton, Gloucestershire, 1959–1964', *Trans. Bristol and Glous. Archaeol. Soc.*, 85 (1966), 83.

30   Taylor, C. C. 'Three Deserted Medieval Settlements in Whiteparish', *W.A.M.*, 63 (1968), 39–45..

31   R.C.H.M., *Dorset* III (1970), Milton Abbas (20); Beresford, M. W. *History on the Ground* (1957), 198–203.

32   Taylor, C. C. *Dorset* (1970), 160–1.

33   Beresford, M. W. and Hurst, J. G. *Deserted Medieval Villages* (1972), 53–6.

34   R.C.H.M., *West Cambridgeshire* (1968), Croxton (16).

35   Taylor, C. C. 'Whiteparish', *W.A.M.* 63 (1967), 92–3.

36   Allison, K. J. *et al. The Deserted Villages of Oxfordshire* (1965); *The Deserted Villages of Northamptonshire* (1966), Univ. of Leics. Dept. Eng. Local Hist. Occ. Paps. 17 and 18.

37   R.C.H.M., *Dorset* III (1970), Stourpaine (7); Taylor C. C. *Dorset* (1970), 111–18.

38   Colvin, H. M. 'Deserted Villages and the Archaeologist', *Arch. Newsletter*, 4 (1952) 129–31; Donkin, R. A. 'Settlement and Depopulation on Cistercian Estates during the Twelfth and Thirteenth Centuries', *Bull. Inst. Hist. Research*,

23 (1960), 141–65; Barley, M. W. 'Cistercian Land Clearances in Nottingham-shire', *Nottingham Medieval Studies*, 1 (1957), 75–89.

39 V.C.H., *North Riding Yorks*, I (1914), 118, 472.

40 Allison, K. J. 'The Lost Villages of Norfolk', *Norfolk Arch.*, 31 (1955), 130–1.

41 Thirsk, J. (Ed.) *The Agrarian History of England and Wales*, IV (1967), 200–55.

42 R.C.H.M., *Dorset* III (1970), Woolland (4).

43 R.C.H.M., *West Cambridgeshire* (1968), 34–5, Caxton (24) and (25).

44 Ravensdale, J. R. 'Landbeach in 1549', in Munby, L. M. (Ed.) *East Anglian Studies* (1968), 94–116.

45 Hall, D. N. and Nickersen, N. 'The Earthworks at Strixton', *Journal of the Northampton Museums and Art Gallery*, 6 (1969), 22–34.

46 R.C.H.M., *West Cambridgeshire* (1968), Papworth St Agnes (2), (9) and (10).

Chapter 8

1 Taylor, C. C. 'Total Archaeology', in Rogers, A. and Rowley, T. (Eds.) *Landscapes and Documents* (1974); Taylor, C. C. 'Whiteparish, The Study of the Development of a Forest Edge Parish', *W.A.M.*, 62 (1967), 79–102.

Select bibliography of medieval and later field monuments

It is impossible to make a complete list of all kinds of medieval and later earthworks which are likely to be found by the diligent field archaeologist. In a work of this length it is not feasible to mention even the characteristic features which should be recognised. In this bibliography a few of the more important or interesting types are listed, with references to books and papers which give useful information and plans for the medieval field archaeologist. These sources often have detailed bibliographies to lead the interested reader further into the particular subject and are in the main not excavation reports but usually the results of fieldwork alone. The bibliography given here is by no means a complete one, nor does it necessarily contain the most recent works on the sites listed.

The perhaps unfortunate concentration in the bibliography of publications by the Royal Commissions and by such workers as Hadrian Allcroft and O. G. S. Crawford is largely an indictment of the lack of medieval fieldwork by the general archaeological world and an indication of what remains to be done.

Castles

a   Armitage, E. S. *The Early Norman Castles of the British Isles*, (1912).
b   Allcroft, A. H. *Earthwork of England,* (1908), 400–52.
c   R.C.A.M. (Wales), *Caernarvonshire* III (1964), cxxxlx–cxliii.
d   Renn, D. F. 'Mottes: A Classification', *Antiquity*, 33 (1959), 106–12.

Churches

a   R.C.H.M. (Eng.), *Dorset* III (1970), Piddletrenthide (39).
b   R.C.A.M. (Scot.), *Stirlingshire* (1963), (160).
c   Beresford, M. W. and St Joseph, J. K. *Medieval England: An Aerial Survey* (1958).

Civil War earthworks of the seventeenth century

a   R.C.H.M. (Eng.), *Newark on Trent: The Civil War Siege Works* (1964).

b O'Neil, B. H. St J. 'A Civil War Battery at Cornbury, Oxford', *Oxoniensia*, 10 (1945), 73–8.
c R.C.H.M. (Eng.), *Huntingdonshire* (1926), Bluntisham cum Earith (3) and Stanground (3).
d R.C.H.M. (Eng.), *Dorset* II (1970), Dorchester (228).
e Allcroft, A. H. op cit., 603–10

Danish earthworks

a Brooks, N. 'The Unidentified Forts of the Burghal Hidage', *Med. Arch.*, 8 (1964), 74–90.
b R.C.H.M. (Eng.), *Dorset* II (1970), Wareham Lady St Mary (79).
c Allcroft, A. H. op cit., 384–90.
d Dyer, J. 'Earthworks of the Danelaw Frontier', in Fowler, P. J. (Ed.) *Archaeology and the Landscape* (1972), 222–36.

Dark Age forts

a R.C.A.M. (Wales), *Caernarvonshire* III (1964), cxv–cxviii.
b R.C.A.M. (Scot.), *Roxburgh* (1956), (16), (145), (201), (307), (459) etc.

Deer parks

a Cantor, L. M. and Wilson, J. D. 'The Medieval Deer Parks of Dorset', *Procs. Dorset Arch. Soc.*, 83 (1961)–91 (1969).
b Peake, H. 'An Earthwork at Ashdown, Berks.', *Trans. Newbury and District F.C.*, 6 (1932), 167–75.
c Crawford, O. G. S. *Archaeology in the Field* (1953), 188–97.

Dovecotes

a *Med. Arch.*, 1 (1957), 619

Enclosures

a R.C.H.M. (Eng.), *Dorset* III (1970), Piddletrenthide (63) and (64).
b Taylor, C. C. 'Late Roman Pastoral Enclosures', *Antiquity*, 41 (1967), 304–6.
c Crawford, O. G. S. and Keiller, A. *Wessex from the Air* (1928), 238.
f Gardner, E. 'A Triple Banked Enclosure on Cobham Common', *Surrey Arch. Coll.*, 35 (1924), 105–13.

Farmsteads, isolated (see also Moats, Shielings and Manorial Sites)

a   Stevenson, R. B. K. 'Medieval Dwelling Sites, Manor, Peebles', *P.S.A.S.,* 75 (1940–1), 92–114.

b   R.C.A.M. (Scot.), *Selkirk* (1957), (76 and 77), (137) and (139).

c   R.C.A.M. (Scot.), *Roxburgh* (1956), (639), (641), (788) and (1032).

d   R.C.H.M. (Eng.), *Dorset* III (1970), Charminster (25).

Fields and field systems

The standard work on agricultural remains of all periods is Bowen, H. C. *Ancient Fields* (1961).

Ridge and furrow

a   Beresford, M. W. 'Ridge and Furrow and the Open Fields', *Econ. Hist. Rev.,* 1 (1948), 34–45.

b   Kerridge, E. 'Ridge and Furrow and Agrarian History', *Econ. Hist. Rev.,* 4 (1951), 14–36.

c   Mead, W. R. 'Ridge and Furrow in Buckinghamshire', *Geog. J.,* 120 (1954), 34–42.

d   Eyre, S. R. 'The Curving Plough Strip and its Historical Implications', *Ag. Hist. Rev.,* 3 (1955), 80–94.

e   R.C.H.M. (Eng.), *West Cambridgeshire* (1968), lxvi–lxix.

f   R.C.A.M. (Scot.), *Stirlingshire* (1963), 51–2.

g   Beresford, M. W. and St Joseph, J. K. op cit., 25–40.

h   Fowler, P. J. and Thomas, A. C. 'Arable Fields of the Pre-Norman Period at Gwithian', *Cornish Arch.,* 1 (1962), 61–84.

Headlands

a   R.C.H.M. (Eng.), *A Matter of Time* (1960), 32.

b   R.C.H.M. (Eng.), *North East Cambridgeshire* (1972), xxxiv.

c   R.C.H.M. (Eng.), *Peterborough New Town* (1968), Alwalton (21).

d   Baker, A. R. H. 'A Relatively Neglected Field Form: The Headland Ridge', *Ag. Hist. Rev.,* 21 (1973), 47–50.

Strip lynchets

a   Taylor, C. C. 'Strip Lynchets', *Antiquity,* 40 (1966), 277–84.

b   R.C.H.M. (Eng.), *Dorset* II (1970), lxix.

c   R.C.H.M. (Eng.), *Herefordshire* III (1934), Aston (5), Aymestry (32), etc.

d   R.C.A.M. (Scot.), *Roxburgh* (1956), (351), (352), (486), (727) and (728).

e   R.C.A.M. (Scot.), *Stirlingshire* (1963), (501), (505) and (507).

f   Graham, A. 'Cultivation Terraces in S.E. Scotland', *P.S.A.S.,* 73 (1938), 289–315.

Narrow rig

a   R.C.H.M. (Eng.), *Dorset* II (1970), lxix.

Water meadows

a   Kerridge, E. 'The Floating of the Wiltshire Water Meadows', *W.A.M.,* 55 (1953), 105–18.
b   Whitehead, J. 'The Management and Land Use of Water Meadows in the Frome Valley, Dorset', *Procs. Dorset Arch. Soc.,* 89 (1967), 251–81.

Lazy beds

a   Evans, E. E. *Irish Folk Ways* (1957), 140–51.
b   R.C.H.M. (Eng.), *Dorset* II (1970), Tyneham (10).

Fields and field patterns

a   Taylor, C. C. 'Medieval and Later Field Shapes in Dorset', *Procs. Dorset Arch. Soc.,* 90 (1969), 249–57.
b   Hewlett, G. 'Reconstructing a Historical Landscape from Field and Documentary Evidence', *Ag. Hist. Rev.,* 21 (1973), 94–110.

Multi-period agricultural remains

a   R.C.H.M. (Eng.), *Dorset* II (1970), Ancient Field Groups 1 and 23.
b   Bowen, H. C. and Fowler, P. J. 'The Archaeology of Fyfield and Overton Downs, Wilts.', *W.A.M.,* 58 (1962), 104–6.

Folds (see also enclosures)

a   Allcroft, A. H. op cit., 231–2.
b   R.C.A.M. (Wales), *Caernarvonshire* I (1956), lxxvii and (324–5).
c   R.C.A.M. (Scot.), *Selkirk* (1957), (157 and 158).
d   R.C.A.M. (Scot.), *Roxburgh* (1956), (50 and 51).
e   Ramm, H. R. 'Survey of an Earthwork at Kingsterndale', *Derby Arch. J.,* 78 (1957), 53.

Gardens

a   R.C.H.M. (Eng.), *West Cambridgeshire* (1968), lxiii, listed under Class B moats.
b   R.C.H.M. (Eng.), *Dorset* IV (1972), Tarrant Gunville (2).

c   R.C.H.M. (Eng.), *Huntingdonshire* (1926), Leighton Bromswold (2); wrongly described as a castle in Beresford, M. W. and St Joseph, J. K. op cit., 14–15.

d   R.C.A.M. (Scot.), *Stirlingshire* (1963), (192).

e   R.C.H.M. (Eng.), *Peterborough New Town* (1969), Longthorpe (7).

Industrial sites

a   Beresford, M. W. and St Joseph, J. K. op cit., 229–42.

b   R.C.A.M. (Scot.), *Stirlingshire* (1963), (561)–(568).

c   Money, J. H. 'Medieval Iron Working in Minepit Wood, Rotherfield, Sussex', *Med. Arch.*, 15 (1971), 86–111.

d   Wrey, E. C. 'Saltpetre House, Ashurst', *Procs. Hants. F.C.*, 21 (1959), 112–13.

Linear earthworks (see also deer parks)

a   Fox, C. *Offa's Dyke* (1955).

b   Fox, A. and C. 'Wansdyke Reconsidered', *Arch. J.*, 115 (1960), 1–48.

c   R.C.H.M. (Eng.), *North East Cambridgeshire* (1972), Appendix.

d   R.C.A.M. (Scot.), *Selkirk* (1957), (178)–(193).

e   R.C.A.M. (Scot.), *Roxburgh* (1956), Appendix.

f   R.C.H.M. (Eng.), *Dorset* II (1970), East Stoke (50).

g   R.C.H.M. (Eng.), *Dorset* III (1970), Winterborne Whitchurch (19).

h   Allcroft, A. H. op cit., 494–522.

Manorial sites (see also farmsteads and moats)

a   R.C.H.M. (Eng.), *Dorset* III (1970), Dewlish (7); Sturminster Newton (69).

Moats

a   Allcroft, A. H. op cit., 453–86.

b   R.C.H.M. (Eng.), *West Cambridgeshire* (1968), lxi–lxvi.

c   Le Patourel, J. 'Moated Sites of Yorkshire', *Chateau Gaillard*, 5 (1970), 121–32.

d   Emery, F. V. 'Moated Settlements in England', *Geography*, 47 (1962), 378–88.

e   Taylor, C. C. 'Moated Sites in Cambridgeshire', in Fowler, P. J. (Ed.) *Archaeology and the Landscape* (1972), 237–49.

f   Roberts, B. K. 'Moated Sites in Midland England', *Trans. Birmingham Arch. Soc.,* 80 (1962), 26–33.

Monastic remains

a   Butler, R. M. 'Wendling Abbey—A Note on the Site', *Norfolk Arch.,* 32 (1960), 226–9.
b   Aston, M. 'The Earthworks of Bordesley Abbey, Redditch, Worcestershire', *Med. Arch.,* 16 (1972), 133–6.
c   Knowles, D. M. and St. Joseph, J. K. *Monastic Sites from the Air* (1952).
d   R.C.H.M. (Eng.), *Huntingdonshire* (1926), Sawtrey Judith (1).
e   R.C.H.M. (Eng.), *North East Cambridgeshire* (1972), Lode (3).

Mounds

Pillow mounds

a   Crawford, O. G. S. and Keiller, A. op cit., 18–24
b   R.C.H.M. (Eng.), *Dorset* II (1970), Church Knowle (29) and Worth Matravers (32).
c   R.C.H.M. (Eng.), *Westmorland* (1936), xxxv; Waitby (16), Ravenstonedale (33), Mallerstang (17).
d   R.C.H.M. (Eng.), *West Cambridgeshire* (1968), Croydon (18).
e   R.C.A.M. (Wales), *Radnorshire* (1913), (327) and (355a).
f   R.C.A.M. (Wales), *Anglesey* (1937), Llanbadrig (7), Llanrhyddlad (3).

Tree mounds

a   R.C.H.M. (Eng.), *Dorset* II (1970), East Holme (12).
b   R.C.H.M. (Eng.), *Dorset* IV (1972), Tarrant Gunville (2).

Windmill mounds

a   Posnansky, M. 'The Langport Post Mill', *Northants. Nat. Hist. Soc.,* 33 (1956), 66–79.
b   Rahtz, P. A. 'A Barrow and Windmill at Butcombe, North Somerset', *Procs. Univ. Bristol Spel. Soc.,* 8 (1958), 89–96.
c   Mortimer, J. *Forty Years Researches . . . in East Yorkshire,* (1905), 187, 206 and 338.
d   Allcroft, A. H. op cit., 534–9 and 645.
e   Beresford, M. W. and St Joseph, J. K. op cit., 65–6.

Pits

a   Prince, H. C. 'The Origins of Pits and Depressions in Norfolk', *Geography,* 49 (1964), 15–32.

Retting pits

a   R.C.H.M. (Eng.), *Monuments Threatened and Destroyed* (1963), 13; South
     Wingfield, Derbyshire.

Ponds

Dew ponds

a   Allcroft, A. H. op cit., 265–86.
b.   Martin, C. A. 'Dew Ponds', *Antiquity*, 4 (1930), 347–51.

Duck decoy ponds

a   Payne-Gallway, R. *The Book of Duck Decoys* (1886).

Fish ponds

a   Allcroft, A. H. op cit., 487–92.
b   Beresford, M. W. and St Joseph J. K. op cit., 68–9.
c   Rahtz, P. A. 'Humberston Earthworks, Leicester', *Trans. Leics. Arch.
     Soc.,* 35 (1959), 1–32.
d   R.C.H.M. (Eng.), *Dorset* III (1970), Shaftesbury (143).
e   R.C.H.M. (Eng.), *North East Cambridgeshire* (1972), Lode (3).

Stock drinking ponds

a   Thompson, O. W. 'The Excavation of Two Moated Sites at Cherry
     Holt near Grantham and at Epperstone near Nottingham', *Reps. and
     Paps. Lincs. Archit. and Arch. Soc.,* 6 (1955), 72–82.

Pottery kilns

a   Le Patourel, J. 'Documentary Evidence and the Medieval Pottery
     Industry', *Med. Arch.,* 12 (1968), 102–26.

Rabbit warrens (see also Pillow mounds)

a   Allcroft, A. H. op cit., 690–1.
b   Haynes, R. G. 'Vermin Traps and Rabbit Warrens on Dartmoor',
     Post Med. Arch., 4 (1970), 147–64.
c   Lineham, C. D. 'Deserted Sites and Rabbit Warrens on Dartmoor',
     Med Arch., 10 (1960), 113–44.
d   Tebbut, C. F. 'Rabbit Warrens in Ashdown Forest', *Sussex Notes and
     Queries,* 17 (1968), 52–7.

Roads and highways

a   Crawford, O. G. S. *Archaeology in the Field* (1952), 67–86.
b   R.C.A.M. (Scot.), *Roxburgh* (1956), 50–1, 477–9, Appendix C.

Salterns

a   Beresford, M. W. and St Joseph, J. K. op cit., 238–42.
b   Thompson, M. W. 'Mounds near Whitstable', *Arch. Cantiana*, 70 (1956), 44–67.

Sheep and cattle shelters

a   Allcroft, A. H. op cit., 554.
b   Hoare, R. C. *Ancient Wilts.* II (1821), 43.
c   Mortimer, J. op cit., 388–96.
d   R.C.H.M. (Eng.), *Herefordshire* I (1931), St Margaret's (7).

Sheep dips

a   Allcroft, A. H. op cit., 231–2.

Shielings or Shiels (see also Farmsteads)

a   Gelling, P. S. 'Medieval Shielings in the Isle of Man', *Med. Arch.,* 6–7 (1962–3), 156–72.
b   R.C.H.M. (Eng.), *Shielings and Bastles* (1970), 1–43.

Stack stands

a   R.C.H.M. (Eng.), *Shielings and Bastles* (1970), 54–60.
b   R.C.A.M. (Scot.), *Roxburgh* (1956), 51.
c   R.C.A.M. (Wales), *Caernarvonshire* III (1964), clxxix–clxxx.

Villages

Deserted medieval villages

a   Allison, K. J. *Deserted Villages* (1970).
b   Beresford, M. W. *The Lost Villages of England* (1954).
c   Beresford, M. W. and Hurst, J. G. *Deserted Medieval Villages* (1971).
d   Beresford, M. W. and St Joseph, J. K. op cit., 16–17, 54–5 and 109–20.

e   Hoskins, W. G. 'Seven Deserted Village Sites in Leicestershire', *Trans. Leics. Arch. Soc.*, 32 (1956), 36–51; reprinted in *Provincial England* (1963), 115–30.

Shrunken or moved villages

a   Beresford, M. W. and St Joseph, J. K. op cit., 107–8.
b   Hall, D. N. and Nickerson, N. 'The Earthworks at Strixton', *Journal of the Northampton Museums and Art Galleries*, 6 (1969), 22–34.
c   R.C.H.M. (Eng.), *Dorset* II (1970), Combe Keynes (12).

Miscellaneous earthworks

Bee gardens

a   Sumner, H. *Earthworks of the New Forest* (1917), 218.

Bowling greens

a   R.C.H.M. (Eng.), *Dorset* II (1970), Wareham Lady St Mary (81).

Cockpits and Bullrings

a   R.C.H.M. (Eng.), *Dorset* III (1970), Iwerne Courtney (17) and Stourpaine (9).

Mazes

Allcroft, A. H. op cit., 602.

Military field kitchens

a   Margary, I. D. 'Military Field Kitchens of the Eighteenth Century', *Sussex Arch. Coll.*, 103 (1965), 60–6.

Pig pens
a   Sumner, H. op cit., 61–8.

Unknown earthworks

a   Crawford, O. G. S. and Keiller, A. op cit., 162–4.
b   R.C.H.M. (Eng.), *Dorset* II (1970), Studland (43).
c   R.C.H.M. (Eng.), *West Cambridgeshire* (1968), Caxton (19).

Useful addresses for medieval field archaeologists

Air Photography Unit, National Monuments Record
Fortress House,
23 Saville Row,
London W1X 1AB

Archaeological Division, Ordnance Survey
Maybush,
Southampton

Archaeology Section, National Monuments Record
Fortress House,
23 Saville Row,
London W1X 1AB

The Council for British Archaeology
8 St Andrew's Place,
London NW1 4LB

Index